YOUTH EMPLOYMENT
AND PUBLIC POLICY

PRENTICE-HALL INTERNATIONAL, INC. (*London*)
PRENTICE-HALL OF AUSTRALIA PTY, LTD. (*Sydney*)
PRENTICE-HALL OF CANADA, LTD. (*Toronto*)
PRENTICE-HALL OF INDIA PRIVATE LIMITED (*New Delhi*)
PRENTICE-HALL OF JAPAN, INC. (*Tokyo*)
PRENTICE-HALL OF SOUTHEAST ASIA PTE., LTD. (*Singapore*)
WHITEHALL BOOKS LIMITED (*Wellington, New Zealand*)

 The American Assembly, *Columbia University*

YOUTH EMPLOYMENT
AND PUBLIC POLICY

Prentice-Hall, Inc., *Englewood Cliffs, New Jersey*

A SPECTRUM BOOK

Library of Congress Cataloging in Publication Data

Main entry under title:

YOUTH EMPLOYMENT AND PUBLIC POLICY.

(A Spectrum Book)
At head of title: The American Assembly,
Columbia University.
    Background papers for the Arden House Assembly
on Youth Employment, Aug. 1979.
    Includes bibliographies and index.
    1. Youth—Employment—United States—Congresses.
2. Minority youth—Employment—United States—
Congresses. 3. Manpower policy—United States—
Congresses. I. American Assembly. II. Arden
House Assembly on Youth Employment, 1979.
HD6273.Y654   331.3′411   79-27022
ISBN 0-13-982413-8
ISBN 0-13-982405-7 pbk.

Editorial/production supervision by Betty Neville
Cover design by Marva Martin
Manufacturing buyer: Barbara A. Frick

10 9 8 7 6 5 4 3 2 1

Table of Contents

Preface   vii

Bernard E. Anderson and
Isabel V. Sawhill
Introduction   1

1 *Richard B. Freeman*
Why Is There a Youth Labor Market Problem?   6

2 *Michael L. Wachter*
The Dimensions and Complexities
of the Youth Unemployment Problem   33

3 *Elijah Anderson*
Some Observations of Black Youth Employment   64

4 *Ernst W. Stromsdorfer*
The Effectiveness of Youth Programs:
An Analysis of the Historical Antecedents
of Current Youth Initiatives   88

5 *Beatrice G. Reubens*
Review of Foreign Experience   112

6 *Bernard E. Anderson and*
Isabel V. Sawhill
Policy Approaches for the Years Ahead   137

Index   157

The American Assembly   163

Preface

It is said that facts speak for themselves. Not always. Nor when they do are they necessarily acted upon to produce the conclusion they seem to request. Here for example is a fact: "the unemployment rate of black youth, exceeding 20 percent for each year during the past quarter century, has risen alarmingly in recent years to over 30 percent . . . similarly the unemployment of Hispanic youth is severe."

Attempts have been made to better understand the problem, and numerous and sincere public policy efforts have been undertaken to reduce it. Yet, for one reason or another, efforts have come up short, and youth unemployment persists at a high level. Facts need people to speak for them.

The book at hand was written on the premise that the nation can ill afford the costs and consequences of this shortcoming, and therefore that more people need to address themselves to the deplorable facts and press harder to find an acceptable consensus on solutions. At present none seems to exist.

The Arden House Assembly on Youth Employment, August 1979, was the beginning of what is hoped will be a "new and major national commitment to alleviating joblessness for young Americans." The final report of that meeting (obtainable by writing The American Assembly) was reached on the basis of the deliberations of seventy-five Americans who used the papers in this volume as background and preliminary guidelines to the issues. But the editors, Bernard E. Anderson of The Rockefeller Foundation and Isabel V. Sawhill, executive director of The National Commission for Employment Policy, fully intended that the chapters should seek a wider reading public and that consideration of them should be accorded a high public priority along with other national goals, including price stability and energy self-sufficiency.

This entire American Assembly project was cosponsored by

the National Commission for Employment Policy. It was financed by the Commission and in part by Carnegie Corporation of New York. But it should be understood that none of these organizations officially endorses the views which follow. Those belong to the authors themselves.

Clifford C. Nelson
President
The American Assembly

Bernard E. Anderson and
Isabel V. Sawhill

Introduction

> *The temptation of the analyst is to treat citizens as objects. By depriving people of autonomy in thought . . . it is possible to deny them citizenship in action. The moral role of the analyst, therefore demands that cogitation enhance the values of interaction and not become a substitute for it.*
>
> Aaron Wildavsky, *Speaking Truth to Power* [1]

The purpose of this volume is to inform citizens, and especially those in a position to act, about the problem of unemployment among the nation's youth. It is just one contribution to

---

ISABEL V. SAWHILL *is the director of the National Commission for Employment Policy. Dr. Sawhill was a principal research associate and director of a program on women and families at The Urban Institute and earlier chaired the Department of Economics at Goucher College. She has written numerous articles and papers and is co-author of the book* Time of Transition: The Growth of Families Headed by Women.

BERNARD E. ANDERSON *is director of the Division of Social Science at The Rockefeller Foundation. Dr. Anderson was a professor at The Wharton School and senior research associate at the Industrial Research Unit, University of Pennsylvania. Aside from numerous articles on economic and labor market policy, he has written four books and most recently co-authored* Moving Ahead: Black Managers in American Business.

[1] Aaron Wildavsky, *Speaking Truth to Power: The Art and Craft of Policy Analysis* (Boston: Little, Brown and Company, 1979), p. 277.

1

what should be a continuing dialogue about this issue, involving all sectors of our society. The authors have focused not only on the dimensions of the problem and its causes, but also on past efforts to deal with it, and likely solutions for the future. To provide a comparative perspective and to guard against too parochial a view, a chapter has been added on the experience of other industrialized countries with youth unemployment. Finally, to ground the discussion in the real world, we have included an account of the attitudes and life styles of those young black men in the urban ghetto who are, literally more often than not, out of work.

While there is nothing new about youth unemployment, there are a number of reasons for reassessing the situation as we enter the decade of the eighties.

First, the baby boom generation has come of age and some stock-taking seems in order. Those born in the 1950s have entered the labor force in the 1970s, testing the capacity of the economic system to make use of their talents and their energies and forcing them, for the first time, to compete in an adult world. Their success, or lack of it, has implications for many of our most basic institutions: the families, schools, and communities which have prepared them for adult roles and the labor market which must now absorb them. One of the themes running through this volume is that these institutions have met the needs of most youth reasonably well; but for a disadvantaged, largely black and increasingly hispanic, minority, the picture is much more disturbing. Using sophisticated quantitative methods economists Richard Freeman and Michael Wachter each identify this group as the core of the problem. Elijah Anderson adds a portrait of some of the individuals hidden behind these impersonal statistics, using his skills as an ethnographer to round out our understanding of the attitudes and behavior patterns of young men from low-income minority families. He attempts to capture the social dynamic of the Civil Rights movement of the sixties, its impact on the consciousness of black youth, and the implications of current black and white attitudes for the job prospects of young black males. From his account, it is not entirely clear when race is more salient than class or how both interact with age, only that all three dimensions seem to be important.

Although most of our authors, including Eli Anderson, give greater attention to young men than to young women, as editors we feel compelled to note that female unemployment rates are higher than those of males for every age-race group. In particular, there is no group more disadvantaged in the labor market than young black women. And, since a surprisingly high proportion of them already have families of their own, their joblessness may well have implications for more than one generation.

A second reason for focusing on youth unemployment is that it is not well understood. Some would say it is not even a problem, just a natural part of maturing which involves some testing of the labor market. Others contend that it is symptomatic of a much deeper and more complex set of interlocking social problems. They argue that it leads to crime, teenage pregnancies, alienation, and impaired life chances for the individuals involved. This is an area where the evidence is thin and certainly less powerful than prior belief.

Even the data on youth unemployment are flawed; different surveys produce different results. Researchers have found that mothers do not always agree with sons on whether the latter are "employed" or "looking for work." But beyond this, the whole concept of what it means to be unemployed has been called into question. There are some who believe the official data overstate the problem because they include those who are voluntarily unemployed while they search—sometimes half-heartedly given their alternative opportunities—for an "acceptable" job. Still others feel that the official measures understate the problem because they do not count those who are so discouraged that they have stopped looking for work altogether.

Once the problem is defined and roughly quantified, there is the further question of its causes. Unemployment among youth can be attributed to a shortage of jobs, or the problem can be blamed on the personal attributes of youth including their inexperience, poor work habits, and basic educational deficiencies. Richard Freeman provides a definitive summary of the relevant research on these issues, concluding that a combination of factors is involved but that a lack of jobs is a major determinant of variation in youth employment over time and among areas. In a similar vein, Beatrice Reubens notes the deep pessimism in many other countries about their ability to absorb new entrants—not only youth but also adult women—into the labor force, given the low growth rates which are forecast for the next decade. Full employment, for young and old alike, is a goal which is as elusive as it is desirable.

This brings us to still a third reason for analyzing youth unemployment as we enter the decade of the eighties. Such an examination represents a turning away from the undifferentiated diagnosis of unemployment and the overreliance on macroeconomic solutions which were so popular in the past. As Michael Wachter indicates in his informative account of the economic events of the sixties, we relied heavily on monetary and fiscal policy during this period and with considerable success. But since then recurring bouts of double digit inflation, which have appeared even when the unemployment rate remained high by historical standards, have necessitated a reassessment of economic policy. Part of this on-going reassessment has involved a focus on the *distribution* of unemployment among groups and a more selective targeting of policy on those groups with the highest unemployment rates. In turning the microscope on youth, this volume is intended not only to help us better understand and meet their needs but also to move us closer to understanding how to achieve broader economic objectives. Youth between the ages of sixteen and twenty-four represent half of those who are unemployed. Thus, there can be no solution to the unemployment problem that does not involve this group.

The fourth and final reason for this volume is the need to reassess what past employment and training programs for youth have accomplished and to sketch out the most promising directions for the future. In his chapter, Ernst Stromsdorfer bemoans the lack of adequate program evaluation in the past and stresses the paucity of hard evidence on what works best and why. Without such evaluations, even the most effective programs are more vulnerable to the latest political whim while ineffective approaches simply become more deeply imbedded in the system. Of course, practitioners —unlike researchers—do not have the luxury of waiting for better solutions to be formulated on the academic drawing boards; nor are they quite as fussy about the quality of the information they use to inform their decisions. However, for those who care to be educated, the record, as slim as it is, is here to be read.

As for the future, there are no simple formulas for success. In the last chapter of this volume the editors attempt to provide some very general principles which might guide the nation's response to the youth employment problem. We caution that realistic expectations about what can be accomplished, a willingness to learn from past mistakes, and better targeting of resources on those most in need are all required if we are to make even modest progress in the years ahead.

In concluding this brief introduction to the volume, we want to express our appreciation to Eli Ginzberg and the other members and staff of the National Commission for Employment Policy who have been so supportive of this project; to Clifford Nelson, who is leaving The American Assembly after more than twenty-five years of exemplary leadership; and to all of the authors for their hard work and intellectual integrity in addressing this difficult topic.

Richard B. Freeman

1

Why Is There
a Youth Labor Market Problem?

Jobless youth have replaced unemployed breadwinners as the focus of concern about unemployment in the United States. Relative to adults, youth have high rates of unemployment, and a smaller proportion of the youth population—including those out of school —is employed. In addition, youth unemployment rates have risen relative to adult unemployment rates while a proportion of youth who are employed has been falling among some groups. This chapter explores the underlying causes of youth joblessness and the reasons for these observed trends.

There are two basic views about the cause of high youth joblessness. According to one view, the principal reason for high and increased joblessness is the lack of adequate demand for young workers due to such factors as slow economic growth; cyclical weaknesses in the economy; changes in the mix of jobs, which alter the level of demand; and minimum wages. According to another view,

Prior to teaching at Harvard University, RICHARD FREEMAN *taught at Yale and the University of Chicago. He is also associated with the National Bureau of Economics Research. Dr. Freeman has written numerous articles for national journals on youth and postcollege employment and one of his books,* Labor Economics, *is in its second edition.*

the principal reason for high and increased youth joblessness is a lack of skills, incentives, and/or aspirations on the part of the young. The two views, while not antithetical, stress different economic forces and lead to different policy recommendations. If the problem is lack of job opportunities, policies to stimulate demand are needed. If the problem lies on the supply side, policies to influence the behavior of youth are needed.

This chapter reviews briefly the patterns and changes in the youth labor market which define the problems to be explained, enumerates the supply and demand factors alleged to underlie the problems, and then examines evidence regarding the quantitative importance of the factors.

The principal results of the analysis can be summarized in five basic propositions:

1. Youth joblessness is concentrated among minority youth and a small segment of white youth and has increased most among minorities, making the problem of causality largely one of explaining the reduced employment of minority youth.

2. Alternative surveys report strikingly different levels of youth work activity, raising major questions about our understanding of the magnitude, much less the nature of the problem, and hampering explanations of causality.

3. Much of the high level of unemployment and nonemployment among young persons can be attributed to normal "life-cycle" patterns of work activity, in which young persons "shop" for appropriate jobs at the outset of working careers, and to institutions which place the burden of adjustment to economic declines on new entrants and persons with low tenure in firms.

4. Because trends in youth joblessness vary by measure and group, it is difficult to determine the causes of the changes in the youth market in the 1970s. On the demand side, employment of youth appears to be highly sensitive to aggregate economic swings, the industrial composition of employment, and somewhat sensitive to the minimum wage; but changes in these forces fail to account for much of observed developments. On the supply side, increased numbers of young persons relative to older persons tend to create problems in the youth market, which show up largely in reductions in the wages of younger as opposed to older workers.

5. While problems with available data leave some issues in

doubt, youth joblessness appears to be due more to lack of jobs than to poor work attitudes or unrealistic wage expectations.

Dimensions of the Problem

Young workers have traditionally exhibited lower levels of work activity than older workers. Labor force participation and employment to population rates are lower for youths than for those twenty-five and over, while rates of unemployment are higher. The earnings and occupational position of the young fall short of the earnings and occupational attainment of older workers. While some of the youth differential is attributable to enrollments in school, out-of-school youth also tend to evince lower propensities to work than adults.

Several important changes in the traditional pattern of youth/ adult labor market differentials in the 1970s have brought the problem of youth joblessness to the center of national attention. Before seeking to explain the causes of the high and/or increasing rate of joblessness among youth, it is important to delineate briefly the principal changes of concern.

Table 1 summarizes developments in the youth labor market in terms of several measures of activity: the percentage of persons with a job (i.e., the employment/population ratio) and the percentage of persons unemployed, disaggregated by age, school status, and race; the ratio of the median weekly earnings of full-time young workers to comparable white male workers twenty-five and over; and the percent of young workers obtaining white-collar jobs. For comparative purposes, the employment/population rate and unemployment rate for older workers are also shown in the table. The table reveals three important aspects about the changing labor market for youth:

1. *The divergent movement of employment/population and unemployment rates for whites.* Line 1 shows that despite great concern with joblessness the percent of white youth holding jobs did *not* decline absolutely or relative to the percent of adults holding jobs in the 1970s. By contrast, line 2 shows an upward trend in rates of unemployment among white youth. Underlying the divergent patterns is an increase in the participation of young whites, especially those in school, in the labor force. One of the principal phenomena to be explained is the concordance of *stability of em-*

ployment/population ratios among white youth with an upward trend in unemployment rates.

2. *The racial dimension of joblessness.* For nonwhite youth both the percent without jobs and the percent unemployed increased in the 1970s, while the rate of labor force participation dropped. *The remarkable decline in the labor force activity of nonwhite youth constitutes the core of the youth joblessness problem.*

3. *The earnings and occupation dimension.* While public attention has focused on the joblessness issue, there have also been major changes in the earnings and occupational position of the young. As line 3 shows, *the earnings of young white men have fallen sharply relative to the earnings of older workers* while those of young blacks have been roughly maintained relative to the earnings of older workers. The drop in the relative earnings of the young constitutes a major shift in age-earnings profiles, with major implications regarding the substitutability between older and younger employees and the flexibility of the wage structure. By contrast, it should be noted that female age-earnings profiles have not undergone much change, possibly because older and younger women are more likely to perform the same type of work.

Finally, line 4 shows that *the fraction of young persons obtaining white-collar jobs has dropped* in the 1970s, reversing a long upward trend in white-collar employment.

What factors explain the higher rates of joblessness among the young and the 1970s changes in youth joblessness and earnings shown in Table 1?

Supply and Demand Factors

The potential causes of high or increasing youth joblessness can be fruitfully analyzed in terms of factors likely to affect joblessness by altering the supply of labor and those likely to affect joblessness by altering the demand for labor. While most measured variables affect both sides of the market, the simple dichotomization provides a useful framework for analysis.

Table 2 sets out the demand and supply views of the effect of major economic variables on employment of youth.

The essential theme of the demand view is that youth joblessness

TABLE 1. DIMENSIONS OF THE YOUTH LABOR MARKET PROBLEM, 1957–1977

	White or Total Male				Black and Other Male			
	1954	1964	1969	1977	1954	1964	1969	1977
1. Percent with job, by age and education								
16–17	40.6	36.5	42.7	44.3	40.4	27.6	28.4	18.9
18–19	61.3	57.7	61.0	65.2	66.5	51.8	51.1	36.9
20–24	77.9	79.3	78.8	80.5	75.9	78.1	77.3	61.2
High school graduates 16–24	—	86.5	88.1	87.0	—	75.8	81.6	67.3
High school dropouts 16–24	—	76.1	74.7	71.1	—	70.3	72.7	50.4
25–54	93.8	94.4	95.1	91.3	86.4	87.8	89.7	81.7
2. Percent of labor force unemployed, by age and education								
16–17	14.0	16.1	12.5	17.6	13.4	25.9	24.7	38.7
18–19	13.0	13.4	7.9	13.0	14.7	23.1	19.0	36.1
20–24	9.8	7.4	4.6	9.3	16.9	12.6	8.4	21.7
High school graduates 16–24	—	8.9	6.0	8.9	—	18.8	11.3	22.0
High school dropouts 16–24	—	13.6	10.8	19.7	—	18.1	12.4	31.5
25–54	3.9	2.8	1.5	3.9	9.5	6.6	2.8	7.8
3. Ratio of weekly earnings of full-time young men to weekly earnings of white men 25 and over			(1967)					
18	—	—	.54	.49	—	—	.44	.44
20	—	—	.66	.58	—	—	.63	.52
22	—	—	.79	.63	—	—	.59	.54
24	—	—	.87	.75	—	—	.60	.63

4. Percent of employed high school graduates not in college and dropouts in white-collar jobs, by year of school leaving, 16–24 years old

	White or Total Female				Black and Other Female			
	1954	1964	1969	1977	1954	1964	1969	1977
Graduate	—	—	20.2	(1976) 14.6				
Dropout	—	—	17.2	7.8				

5. Percent with job, by age

	White or Total Female				Black and Other Female			
	1954	1964	1969	1977	1954	1964	1969	1977
16–17	25.8	25.3	30.3	37.5	19.8	12.5	16.9	12.5
18–19	47.2	43.0	49.2	54.3	29.9	32.9	33.7	28.0
20–24	41.6	45.3	53.3	61.4	43.1	43.7	51.5	45.4
25–54	40.1	41.0	46.2	54.1	49.0	52.7	56.3	57.4

6. Percent of labor force unemployed, by age

	White or Total Female				Black and Other Female			
	1954	1964	1969	1977	1954	1964	1969	1977
16–17	12.0	17.1	13.8	18.2	19.1	36.5	31.2	44.7
18–19	9.4	13.2	10.0	14.2	21.6	29.2	25.7	37.4
20–24	6.4	7.1	5.5	9.3	13.2	18.3	12.0	23.6
25–54	5.0	4.3	3.2	5.8	8.3	8.4	5.0	9.8

7. Percent of employed high school graduates not in college, in white-collar jobs, by years of school leaving, 16–24 years

	White or Total Female				Black and Other Female			
	1954	1964	1969	1977	1954	1964	1969	1977
			(1967) 65.8	(1976) 52.0				

Sources: Items 1 and 5 from U.S. Department of Labor, *Employment and Training Report of the President, 1978,* Tables A–3, A–4 and A–14 (pp. 183–185, pp. 186–188 and pp. 202–204);

Item 6 from U.S. Department of Labor, *Employment and Training Report of the President, 1978,* Tables A–20 and A–3 (pp. 213–214 and pp. 183–185);

Item 3 from U.S. Bureau of Census, May CPS tapes unpublished tabulation;

Items 4 and 7, U.S. Department of Labor, *Handbook of Labor Statistics, 1977,* Table 30, p. 76.

Note: White for all items except lines 4 and 7.

TABLE 2. TWO VIEWS OF THE CAUSES OF YOUTH JOBLESSNESS

Youth Jobless- ness Is High because of:	Demand View	Supply View
Availability of jobs	There is a shortage of jobs for young persons due to aggregate economic forces.	There are many unfilled low-level jobs.
Wages	Minimum wages and other rigidities reduce the number of low-level jobs.	Young persons have unrealistic wage aspirations.
Turnover	Short-term temporary jobs underlie high rates of joblessness.	Young workers are unstable and highly mobile.
Attitudes	Youth desire jobs with a future. Employer discrimination reduces demand for young workers.	At current levels of income, youth prefer leisure and lack the work ethic.
Skills	Skills are learned on the job.	Youth lack education and skills.
The baby boom cohort	The labor market generates many new jobs for young persons, as occurs each summer.	Youth joblessness is due partly to the enormous increase in the size of the youth population.
Alternative "work" activities	Youth have high earnings from illegal "underground" economic activity.	

results from a shortage of jobs either in total or of the "appropriate" type.

One reason for the lack of jobs is that demand is depressed by legislated minimums and other noncompetitive forces which raise youth wages above market clearing levels. The minimum is alleged to have an especially deleterious effect on the availability of "learning jobs," defined as those providing on-the-job training, since youths cannot "purchase" training with low wages.

Another potential reason for a job shortage is the sluggish growth of the aggregate economy which, given institutions like seniority that protect older workers from layoffs, takes an especially harsh toll on employment of new, younger workers.

Changes in the structure of demand, ranging from technological developments to the declining share of agriculture, which traditionally employs relatively many young men, are also likely causes of inadequate demand.

With respect to types of jobs, the existence of many short-term but temporary jobs, including those on short-term work projects, is alleged to contribute to high youth unemployment rates. This is because when short-term jobs end some employees become unemployed while searching for new positions.

Finally, employer discrimination against youth, particularly minority youth, is another potential cause of joblessness.

The supply view stresses the attitudes and skills of youth in the job market. It is not the lack of jobs but the unwillingness of the young to accept those that are available for persons of their skills that is the prime cause of the joblessness problem. Youths are alleged to have excessive wage aspirations, high turnover, poor education and skill, and a lack of the work ethic.

Excessive wage aspirations imply that young persons reject low-wage jobs, preferring to be unemployed than to work, say as a $3.50 per hour dishwasher or busboy, despite lack of skills. If youth have excessive wage aspirations, increases in the minimum wage might increase youth participation rates and possibly youth employment as well—contrary to the prediction of the demand analysis.

The "naturally" high turnover of young workers is a key element in the supply analysis. On the one hand, the young are expected to exhibit high rates of mobility as they "shop" for jobs in what some view as an efficient way of searching for a relatively permanent career. On the other hand, some of the high turnover is alleged to reflect unstable work habits, partially induced by the nature of low-level labor markets.

The supply analysis also puts great weight on the inadequate education, skill, and motivation of the young. Some stress the quality of formal education, in particular the often outmoded and weak vocational courses. Others focus on the failure of the educational system to provide adequate counseling and placement. Others stress the poor cognitive skills of the young and the absence of the work ethic.

While by no means necessarily antithetical and indeed in some cases complementary, the demand and supply views offer very different perspectives on the youth labor market problem and on the policies that might improve the situation. From the demand perspective, what is needed is to generate additional jobs for youth by stimulating the employer side of the market. From the supply perspective, the need is to alter youth attitudes and skills by activities that affect the youth themselves.

One additional potential cause of high youth joblessness, which could be classified as reflecting demand for youth services in other markets or reduced supply in the labor market, also deserves attention. This is the possibility that joblessness is high because youth face attractive alternatives in illegal or "underground" economic activities.

Causes of Increasing Problems

The evidence in Table 1 shows not only that youth have higher rates of joblessness and lower pay than older workers but that their disadvantage has increased in several respects: the percentage without jobs has grown among black and white high school dropouts; the percentage unemployed has risen modestly; the relative earnings of the young have dropped sharply. What might explain these trends?

There are three major explanatory hypotheses relating to demand forces:

1. The demand for young workers has increased too slowly because of: slow economic growth; cyclical conditions; and structural changes in the mix of jobs by industry, occupation, and area.
2. Expanded coverage of the minimum wage and related increases in the cost of hiring labor have reduced the number of youth jobs along given demand curves.
3. Increased supplies of competitive labor, notably adult women and illegal aliens, have reduced the demand for young workers.

On the supply side, the trends in youth unemployment and joblessness may be attributable to:

4. The enormous increase in the relative number of young workers due to

the baby boom cohort has required sizable market adjustments, some of which are not attainable in the relevant period.

5. Increased family incomes and welfare funds, and greater willingness of parents and community to support not employed youth have induced the young to choose "leisure."

6. Deleterious social developments—increased one parent/female homes, inner city community problems, deteriorated quality of schooling, drug usage, and crime—have made the young less employable than in the past.

To offer a valid explanation of youth market developments, these hypotheses must explain the strikingly different levels and trends in joblessness and relative earnings among young blacks and whites. As there is probably some truth to each hypothesis, the problem is not one of determining which is "right" or "wrong" but rather of evaluating their quantitative contribution to the observed changes.

Evidence

Several sources of data on the youth labor market can be used to analyze the cause of high or increasing rates of joblessness:

1. time series evidence, published by the Bureau of Labor Statistics, which shows how youth employment, wages, or unemployment and various explanatory factors vary on an annual, quarterly, or monthly basis;

2. cross-sectional data on individuals from the major governmental survey of households, the Current Population Survey (CPS), which provides the basic economic intelligence used to evaluate youth joblessness but suffers from being based on the responses of adults in the households rather than on the responses of the young persons themselves;

3. longitudinal data on individuals from panel surveys, which are obtained from interviews with the youths and which follow the progress of an individual over time. The longitudinal data have the advantage of permitting the analyst to isolate the effect of social factors of concern from "unmeasured" attributes of individuals by comparing the behavior of the same individuals over time;

4. cross-area evidence, which shows how differences in city or state characteristics lead to bigger or smaller youth labor market problems. A standard research strategy is to estimate the effect of explanatory factors on a particular outcome using cross-area data and then to use the estimates and evidence on changes in the explanatory factors to try to account for changes over time in the dependent variables;

5. evidence from firms, which provides information on the personnel and
   employment practices of firms and thus on demand behavior, but which
   is gathered only relatively infrequently and used sparsely in analyses of
   youth labor market problems.

Comparisons of the picture of the youth labor market given by
the different sources of data have turned up one major problem that
significantly mars efforts to measure the magnitudes, much less the
cause, of high or rising joblessness. The problem is that the fraction
of youth employed differs greatly between the Current Population
Survey and the longitudinal surveys. In particular, the percent of
youth with jobs is much higher in the longitudinal surveys than in
the Current Population Survey. The National Longitudinal Survey,
for example, shows 46 percent of sixteen to seventeen year old men
employed in 1966 compared to a 36 percent figure for the CPS
(Freeman and Medoff in Freeman and Wise). The longitudinal
surveys also show smaller black-white differences in the percent
with jobs than are shown in the CPS.

One reason for this divergence appears to be differences in who
responds to the survey. When young persons respond themselves,
they are more likely to report working than when their parent or
other adults tell an interviewer about youth activity. Another reason may be that the longitudinal surveys contain a more stable
group of young persons. What is important to remember is that
until the discrepancy in survey results is resolved and the "correct"
rate of youth employment determined there will be ambiguity about
the causes of the problem as well.

Given this proviso, what can be said about the reasons for high
rates of joblessness among youth and for increases in the severity
of the problem over time?

Why Youth Joblessness Is High

Annual rates of activity, such as the percentage of the labor
force that is unemployed or the percentage of the population with
a job, depend on three factors: the fraction of persons in the state
of unemployment over a year, the average number of spells or times
each of those persons is in the state, and the average length of spells
measured as a percentage of time over the year. When the fraction
of persons in the state rises, when the number of times a person is

in the state rises, or when the length of time in the state rises, the annual rate rises. Algebraically this is stated as:

$$
\begin{array}{c} Annual \\ Rate\ in \\ State \end{array} = \begin{array}{c} percentage \\ of\ persons \\ in\ state \\ over\ year \end{array} \times \begin{array}{c} number\ of \\ spells\ per \\ person\ in \\ state \end{array} \times \begin{array}{c} average\ length \\ of\ spells\ as \\ fraction\ of\ year \\ (=average\ weeks/52) \end{array}
$$

Analyses of the difference between the rates of unemployment of young and older persons show most of the differences in unemployment rates attributable to *differences in the percentage of persons who experience unemployment over the year* rather than to differences in spells per person or in the length of spells. In 1974, for example, 32 percent of sixteen to nineteen year olds out of school experienced some unemployment, averaging nineteen weeks over the year, compared to 13 percent of workers twenty years and over who had some unemployment for an average of sixteen weeks of unemployment over the year (Clark and Summers in Freeman and Wise). Understanding teenage unemployment requires an explanation of: (a) why young persons are so much more prone to being in the state of unemployment and (b) why they do not spend that much more time in unemployment than other workers.

One major reason for teenagers having such a high probability of being unemployed over the year is that they are new entrants to the labor force (see Table 3). In 1978, 47 percent of unemployed white sixteen to seventeen year olds and 54 percent of unemployed black sixteen to seventeen year olds never worked before compared to just 3 percent of unemployed men twenty years and over. An additional third of unemployed sixteen to seventeen year olds were categorized as reentrants—persons who were reported to have left the labor force in one month, returning for work in the next. Among eighteen to nineteen year olds, the proportion of entrants and reentrants among the unemployed was smaller but still sizable. By contrast, the rates of unemployment of teenagers due to having lost their job via a layoff or having left a job via a quit are more moderately above the rates for adult men. Part of the high unemployment rate is due to the process by which young persons enter the world of work for the first time. In the U.S., *but not* in all countries, entry into the work force often involves a period of unemployment while searching for work. In the United Kingdom, by

TABLE 3. DIRECT CAUSES OF YOUTH UNEMPLOYMENT [1]

Age and Status	White				Black			
	1969	1975	1978[2]	1978[2]	1969	1975	1978[2]	1978
16–17		Rates of Unemploy- ment		Frac- tion of Un- em- ploy- ment		Rates of Unemploy- ment		Frac- tion of Un- em- ploy- ment
Total Unem- ployment	12.5	19.7	19.7	100.0	24.6	39.2	46.4	100.0
Losers	1.6	3.4	3.2	16.2	2.1	4.8	4.5	9.7
Leavers	1.0	1.4	1.2	6.1	1.6	1.1	1.4	3.0
Total entrants	9.9	15.0	15.3	77.7	20.9	33.9	40.8	87.9
Reentrants	4.3	5.9	6.1	31.0	10.2	15.3	15.7	33.8
New entrants	5.6	9.0	9.2	46.7	10.7	18.5	25.1	54.1
18–19								
Total unem- ployment	7.9	17.1	13.4	100.0	18.8	32.9	33.5	100.0
Losers	2.0	8.1	5.4	40.3	5.9	13.0	10.2	30.4
Leavers	1.5	1.7	1.8	13.4	3.3	2.3	2.6	7.8
Total entrants	4.5	7.2	6.2	46.3	10.0	17.9	20.7	61.8
Reentrants	3.0	4.3	3.7	27.6	7.0	10.1	10.6	32.5
New entrants	1.5	3.0	2.5	18.7	3.0	7.5	10.2	30.4
20–24								
Total Unem- ployment	4.6	13.0	10.7	100.0	8.4	23.0	22.8	100.0
Losers	1.8	8.6	6.2	57.9	3.9	14.9	11.4	50.0
Leavers	0.9	1.4	1.9	17.8	1.7	1.4	1.6	7.0
Total entrants	1.9	3.2	2.6	24.3	2.7	6.7	9.8	43.0
Reentrants	1.7	2.7	2.2	20.6	1.8	4.8	7.3	32.0
New entrants	0.3	0.5	0.4	3.7	0.9	1.9	2.5	11.0

[1] Unemployment weighted counts are taken from unpublished data provided by BLS. Labor force numbers are taken from *Employment and Training Report of the President*, 1977, Table A–8 (pp. 139–143).

[2] 1978 percentages are unweighted averages of percentages for the first three months of 1978.

contrast, institutional factors—the Career Services system for young persons and apprenticeship programs—tend to produce low entry rate unemployment.

The reason why young persons have about as lengthy spells of unemployment as older persons is, as Marston and Clark and Summers have pointed out, due to the fact that teenagers tend to drop out of the labor force, or be reported as dropping out, when they become unemployed. When spells out of the labor force and spells of unemployment are added together to obtain spells of *nonemployment*, young persons are found to be out of work for longer periods than adults.

Decomposition of employment/population ratios for younger and older workers shows even greater differences in the lengths of employment spells between young and older workers, with an average completed spell of employment of teenagers (which may include changes in jobs without moving into nonemployment) much below those for all workers twenty and over.

An alternative way of demonstrating the way the short length of youth jobs contributes to the age differential in unemployment is to decompose the rate of unemployment for persons in the work force into the probability of unemployment given a job change multiplied by the probability of a job change. The chances of being unemployed, given a change, are the same as for older workers. Differences in unemployment reflect differences in the proportion of persons who are job changers: about one-fourth of men eighteen to twenty-four change jobs in a year compared to less than one-tenth of thirty-five to fifty-four year olds (see Mincer and Leighton in Freeman and Wise). The differential proportion of job changers by age is itself largely attributable, according to Mincer and Leighton's calculations, to differences in seniority by age. Low-seniority workers, of necessity primarily young workers, change jobs frequently while high-seniority workers, of necessity primarily older workers, change less frequently and are, as a result, less likely to be unemployed.

We conclude that one of the key factors behind high youth joblessness is the high mobility and short tenure of the young.

Incidence

Joblessness is concentrated among certain groups of young persons and is relatively infrequent among others. Studies of the effect of diverse socioeconomic factors on the probability that young persons will be employed show that with diverse other factors held fixed:

1. Black youth have a lower probability of employment. Among teens this is largely due to problems in obtaining a first job upon entry into the market. Among twenty to twenty-four year olds higher chances of being laid off contribute to the lower probability.
2. Youth from disadvantaged areas, notably those where relatively many families have incomes below the poverty level, also have lower probabilities of employment.
3. Youth with less schooling, such as high school dropouts, tend to be markedly prone to joblessness.
4. Youth living in areas where there are relatively many young persons tend to suffer greater joblessness than other youth.
5. Youth living in areas where the mix of industries is favorable to employment of the young (i.e., with many service and trade establishments), where economic growth is rapid, and where adult unemployment is relatively low tend to have higher rates of employment than other youth.
6. Surprisingly, perhaps, with the exception of those from homes below the poverty level, youth from low-income families do not have noticeably lower chances of holding a job than youth from high-income families.
7. Youth working in certain occupations, those with high initial wages but slow wage growth, and in industries in which the work force tends to be highly mobile, have higher rates of unemployment.

As a result of the high concentration of youth joblessness among blacks and selected groups of whites, much youth joblessness is attributable to a *small "hard core" of young people* who experience many weeks without work. Over half of unemployment among male teenagers out of school has been estimated as due to the unemployment of persons with more than six months of unemployment (Clark and Summers).

The factors that are associated with youth joblessness are not, it is important to recognize, the same factors that determine the wages of young workers. Being black, in particular, reduces the probability of holding a job but does *not* substantially affect the wages of the young. The major economic surveys of youth in the 1970s, ranging from the Survey of Income and Education (based on an expanded Current Population Survey sample) to the National Longitudinal Survey of the High School Class of 1972 show that, conditional on other factors, white and black youth have essentially the same wages.

ESTIMATED PERCENTAGE EFFECT OF BEING BLACK ON WAGES, 1972–76

All young men, from Survey of Income and Education, 1975	*Percent*
16–17	.14
18–19	−.06
20–24	−.05
Young men in high school class of 1972, by year	
1972	.02
1973	.02
1974	.01
1975	.05
1976	.04

Sources: Meyer & Wise in Freeman and Wise; Freeman in Freeman and Wise.

Other measures of family background which appear to reduce employment probabilities—such as coming from homes on welfare—also have little impact on wages. By contrast, parental income, which is only weakly associated with youth unemployment, has a sizable effect on youth wages, suggesting that the wealthy are able to help their children obtain better jobs.

Jobs versus People

To what extent is youth joblessness due to lack of jobs as opposed to lack of skills or motivation among people?

Since employment and wages depend both on supply and demand forces, the job versus people question, which dominates much popular discussion of youth unemployment, is in one sense poorly posed. What can be examined is the extent to which variation in some of the supply and demand factors listed in Table 2 affect the level of joblessness, conditional on the level of the other factors.

With respect to jobs, a strong case can be made that lack of jobs is a major contributor to youth joblessness, in the sense that increased demand for youth labor, at existing wages or possibly even at lower wages, will in fact greatly increase youth employment. The evidence for this claim is several fold.

First, virtually every study of youth employment shows substantial responsiveness of the number working to aggregate economic conditions. Changes in the unemployment rate of prime-age men are invariably found to have enormous effects on the employment/population ratio, participation rate, and unemployment rate of youth, especially nonwhite youth. As an example of the magnitude of the response to cyclical changes, consider the following estimates of the effect of a change in the total male unemployment rate on youth male employment/population ratios.

EFFECT OF PERCENTAGE POINT INCREASE IN TOTAL MALE UNEMPLOYMENT
ON YOUTH EMPLOYMENT/POPULATION RATIOS, BY AGE

Based on	16–17 Year Olds	18–19 Year Olds	20–24 Year Olds
Time series	−2.1	−1.7	−3.4
Cross-section	−2.4	−2.3	−1.5

Source: Freeman in Freeman and Wise.

Estimates of the cyclic responsiveness of black youth employment/population ratios suggest responsiveness about 50 percent higher than the figures for all youth. Such significant cyclic responsiveness would be unlikely in the absence of a substantial shortfall of youth jobs when the economy is in a downturn. Corroboratory evidence from comparisons of Standard Metropolitan Statistical Areas (SMSA) shows a similar pattern: the major determinant of employment/population differences across SMSAs is the level of aggregate demand in the SMSA.

Second, several studies of unemployed youth (as well as of other unemployed workers) have found that *virtually no unemployed young job seeker reports having rejected a job offer during the period of search.* If there were not a shortage of jobs, we would expect the unemployed to be picking and choosing, engaged in the process of searching for the best offer, but in fact that does not appear to be the case: most get no job offers at all. Similarly, comparisons of the "reservation wage" of young workers—the wage at which the young claim they would accept a job—with actual wages received gives little indication that, were additional youth jobs available, there would be insufficient applicants.

One frequent objection to the shortage of jobs hypothesis is that newspapers, store windows, employment agencies, and the like are often bursting with help-wanted ads. A 1978 *Fortune* magazine study of actual want ads has effectively demolished this argument. The *Fortune* researchers found that of 228 ads in the help-wanted section of a newspaper, only 142 represented real job offerings within commuting range of the city and, of those, only forty-two did not require special skills. The employers offering those forty-two jobs were "fairly swamped by a tidal wave of applicants." While turnover of workers and jobs guarantees continual openings, the number of jobs falls far short of the number of plausible applicants.

To what extent can the lack of jobs for youth be attributed to the minimum wage? With rare exception, studies of the effect of the minimum wage on youth employment suggest that the minimum reduces youth employment by moderate amounts but may have larger effects on black than white youth. A 10 percent increase in the minimum relative to average wages is usually found to reduce youth employment by somewhere between 1 percent to 4 percent (Gramlich, Mincer, Ragan). This implies that recent increases may have reduced youth employment by perhaps 2 percent to 6 percent. Because reduction in the minimum would raise the labor force as well as employment, however, the effects on youth unemployment rates are much less: the recent increases may have increased the youth unemployment rate by no more than 2 to 3 percentage points.

The nature as well as the number of jobs available to youth also appears to affect the rate of joblessness. Analysis of the effect of occupation on youth unemployment shows that, with diverse personal characteristics fixed, youths in what may reasonably be characterized as "dead end" jobs tend to have higher rates of unemployment than other youths (Brown in Freeman and Wise). Increasing the number of youth jobs will reduce youth unemployment but increasing the number of jobs with a future is likely to have a greater impact on youth joblessness than increasing the number of dead-end jobs.

Finally, it is important to recognize that at least some of the lack of jobs for youth may be attributed to explicit employer personnel policies. Surveys of company hiring practices in the past have revealed definite employer preferences against younger workers, which may or may not be economically justifiable on the basis of differential productivity, wage, and turnover costs. One study, for example, found that in 1970 about 80 percent to 90 percent of employers preferred workers twenty-two years or older, compared to those under twenty-two, even for relatively low-level jobs (Diamond and Bedrosian). While age discrimination laws have induced some firms to drop age from application forms, it is still likely that most enterprises prefer older employees. At present we lack the detailed information on productivity, labor costs, and turnover and training to determine whether these preferences are rational or discriminatory.

For black youths, of course, there is an additional problem: at least some employers, despite the equal opportunity laws, may be less willing to hire black than white youth, possibly for reasons of communication across cultural lines as well as prejudice. High levels of youth crime in some inner cities could also lead to employers being fearful of hiring black youth.

That there is a definite shortage of jobs for young persons does not mean that there are no "people" problems. Youth joblessness is, as noted earlier, concentrated among a small group of persons, a large fraction of whom are black. Expansion of aggregate demand would raise their employment, but levels of joblessness are so high as to suggest other problems as well. While definitive evidence is lacking, many believe that broad socioeconomic community problems in inner cities—where poverty, poor schooling, broken homes, drug and alcohol abuse, out-of-wedlock births, and crime are rampant—contribute significantly to the problem of youth employment. On the one hand, many of these youths lack the affective and cognitive skills required for jobs in the regular economy. On the other, various illegal activities may offer a sizable source of potential earnings. Even at cyclical peaks, these youth tend to have relatively high joblessness and unemployment rates.

In sum, the empirical evidence suggests that while much of youth joblessness is associated with turnover and mobility, alternative institutional arrangements could reduce unemployment due to initial job search, and, while lack of jobs is critical, for the groups with the highest rate of joblessness there are additional "people" problems.

Causes of Change

Because of the diverse developments in the youth labor market documented in Table 1, it is more difficult to explain things over time. Some of the observed patterns of change appear to be explicable by the hypotheses outlined earlier. Others, however, remain a mystery.

The change that seems to be the easiest to explain is the decline in the wages of young workers relative to older workers. Estimates of the substitutability of workers by age suggest that large increases in the relative number of young men (but not young women) will reduce their wages compared to those of older workers. On the basis of these estimates, much of the decline in the relative earnings of the young can be attributed to the enormous influx of the baby boom generation onto the job market. If this interpretation is correct, the relative wages of the young will rise in the 1980s as their relative supply declines.

The decline in youth wages relative to adult wages (see line 3, Table 1) may help explain one of the puzzles of the 1970s: the fact that despite such adverse developments as a rise in the adult male unemployment rate, increased relative numbers of some young age groups (twenty to twenty-four year olds), and extended coverage of the minimum rate, youth employment and employment/population rates rose in the 1970s. From 1969 to 1977, for example, the number of teenage employed workers increased by 28 percent while the number of twenty to twenty-four year olds employed increased by 38 percent. One possible explanation consistent with the observed wage patterns is that the minimum notwithstanding, the relative wages of youth fell sufficiently as to generate a sizable number of jobs. Because youth participation rose (for reasons that have not been explored in detail), the rate of youth unemployment increased despite the growth of employment.

While analytically intriguing, the greater than expected 1970s increase in youth employment is not, of course, the reason for societal concern with youth joblessness. The reason for concern is the increased relative joblessness among black youth. From 1969 to 1977, while white teenage employment increased, black teenage employment actually fell by 3.1 percent. Which of the hypotheses described earlier accounts for the reduction in the ratio of the employment/population rate for black youths and for the increase in the ratio of black to white youth unemployment rates?

No clear answer exists at present. Extant studies suggest that some of the proposed factors have contributed to the change, but the studies fall short of explaining the striking deterioration in the position of black youth.

On the demand side, sluggish aggregate conditions, as reflected in the prime age male unemployment rate, have added to black youth joblessness. Roughly, the two point increase in the prime age (thirty-five to forty-four year olds) male rate from 1969 to 1977 lowered the employment/population rate of black youth by twelve points and by seven points relative to its impact on the comparable ratio for white youth. Similarly, the increased relative number of black youth may have reduced their employment/population ratio in the 1970s. The puzzle remains, however, as to why white youth employment managed to rise despite these developments while black youth employment did not.

The hypothesis that some of the black youth employment reflects suburbanization of jobs has some validity. High rates of joblessness among black youth in suburbia, however, show that this factor can only be a minor contribution to the adverse trends. Only 24 percent of black teenagers living in suburbs held jobs in 1975 compared to 47.2 percent of white teenagers. Teenage unemployment rates for blacks outside of central cities, while smaller than those in central cities, exceeded those of white teenagers in central cities. If all blacks lived outside metropolitan areas, their unemployment rate would still be in the 30 percent range (Westcott).

Reduction in the size of the military, which can be viewed as a drop in demand for labor which makes extensive use of blacks, represents another possible cause of the downward trend in the percent of black youths with a job. Because the black share of the military rose sharply after Vietnam, however, it is difficult to attribute more than a small fraction of the seventies downward trend in black youth employment to the drop in the size of the military.

The possibility that black youth employment has been adversely affected by wage developments deserves greater attention. As shown in Table 1, the decline in the relative wages of youth was concentrated among whites. To the extent that the increased wage of blacks is due to the minimum wage or increased antibias governmental activity which raises wages along existing demand curves, some of the reduced black employment could be attributed to the improved wages. What proportion is so attributable has not yet been determined.

While often cited as a possible cause of increased youth unemployment, the influx of illegal aliens, who might be especially good substitutes for less skilled minority youth, has also not been evaluated quantitatively. Limited work on the effect of increased female participation on youth employment shows little evidence that youths have been adversely affected by the growth of the female work force (Freeman in Freeman and Wise). This raises doubts that increased numbers of aliens have reduced youth employment as well.

Inability to explain the pattern of black youth joblessness in terms of changes in labor demand has directed attention toward the various supply hypotheses listed in Table 2.

The major supply side development—the enormous increase in the relative number of young workers due to the baby boom cohort—has been cited by some as an important factor in the reduced employment chances of young blacks, largely because of the greater increase in the number of black than of white youth. If employers discriminate on the basis of race, the greater increase in the number of young blacks could be expected to have an especially adverse effect on their employment chances, particularly given the increase in the wages of black relative to white youth. Calculations by Wachter (in Freeman and Wise) show sizable effects of the increased number of young persons on black employment/population ratios. While the population trend appears to contribute to explaining the observed drop in employment/population for blacks, Wachter does not believe that it accounts for the bulk of the change.

With respect to parental and community support of jobless youth, the evidence does not tell a clear story. On the one hand, while there is some support for the argument that increased welfare funds have reduced employment of inner city youth, and while families

Richard B. Freeman

on welfare have increased, the effect of being on welfare on youth employment is not large enough to account for the trend in joblessness. Similarly, given the rough stability in real family incomes—as distinct from individual earnings—it is difficult to argue that increased affluence among the poor accounts for reduced youth work.

On the other hand, part of the reduction in the black employment/population ratio is related to the increase in black enrollment in school shown below:

PATTERNS OF ENROLLMENT AMONG YOUNG MALES

	Percent Enrolled in School (Black)			*Percent Enrolled in School (White)*		
	16–17	*18–19*	*20–24*	*16–17*	*18–19*	*20–24*
1964	84.3	39.9	8.3	90.4	52.4	25.6
1969	87.4	49.5	20.5	92.2	60.9	33.2
1977	92.5	50.6	26.1	89.5	47.7	25.7

As a result of the increased enrollment of blacks, the employment/population rate of sixteen to seventeen year old blacks would have fallen (assuming no change in participation rates of enrolled and not enrolled youths) by two points from 1969 to 1977; the employment/population rate of eighteen to nineteen year old blacks would have fallen by one point, while the rates for twenty to twenty-four year olds would have fallen by two points. Since the white enrollment ratios fell over this period, the increased tendency for blacks to choose school helps explain the differential pattern of change by race.

Evidence on the effect of deleterious social developments on the employability of inner city youth, while scattered, tends to suggest a major problem. There is no doubt that drug abuse, alcoholism, youth crime, and related activities which reduce employability plague inner city youth. Limited time series data show marked upward trends in these and other indicators of the status of youth. Similarly, few would disagree with the oft-expressed complaint that quality of education is often quite poor in inner cities, although whether quality has deteriorated in recent years is open to question.

Limited evidence on attitudes shows that black youths from northern urban backgrounds are less committed to work than black youths from southern backgrounds, and that these differences are a factor in labor market achievement.

While it is difficult to differentiate cause from effect, there does appear to be a significant employability problem among inner city youths which contributes to the trend in joblessness.

Conclusion

The preceding analysis of the causes of youth joblessness and related labor market problems suggests that much remains to be learned. Partly because of inconsistencies in reported rates of youth employment across surveys and partly because of problems in measuring key social variables, it is difficult to reach firm conclusions. As far as can be told, much of the relatively high rate of youth joblessness can be attributed to turnover and mobility patterns that are normal in the U.S. economy, but much is also directly related to a dearth of jobs. Demand forces, which have come to be neglected in favor of supply in much popular discussion of youth joblessness, are major determinants of variation in youth employment over time and among areas. For groups facing the most severe joblessness problem, however, the difficulty due to lack of jobs appears to be compounded by problems of employability related to deleterious social patterns. Surprisingly, perhaps, the factors that determine the probability that young persons end up employed or jobless differ substantively from those that determine wages.

While we have been able to explain the decline in the earnings of young workers relative to the earnings of older workers in the 1970s, the causes of the divergent trend in youth employment between all young persons and nonwhites remain a conundrum. For reasons that are unclear, white youth employment/population ratios have stabilized or risen in the period, despite adverse economic developments, while black youth employment/population ratios have been dropping since the mid-1950s. While these trends are likely to have been influenced by the wage patterns, shifts in demand, and various social developments, no definitive accounting exists at present. The causes of the divergent trends have been illuminated but not resolved by existing work.

Bibliography

ADIE, D. K., and L. GALLOWAY, "The Minimum Wage and Teenage Unemployment," *Western Economic Journal* (December 1973).

COLEMAN, JAMES S., "The School to Work Transition," *The Teenage Unemployment Problem: What are the Options?*, Congressional Budget
Office (October 14, 1976).

COTTERHILL, PHILIP G., and WALTER J. WADYCKI, "Teenagers and the
Minimum Wage in Retail Trade," *Journal of Human Resources* (winter
1976).

DIAMOND, DANIEL E., and HRACH BEDROSIAN, *Industry Hiring Requirements and the Employment of Disadvantaged Groups.* New York: New
York University School of Commerce, 1970.

DUNCAN, BEVERLY, "Dropouts and the Unemployed," *Journal of Political
Economy* (April 1965).

FREEMAN, RICHARD B., "Teenage Unemployment: Can Reallocating Educational Resources Help?" *The Teenage Unemployment Problem: What
Are The Options?*, Congressional Budget Office (October 14, 1976).

————, "The Effect of Demographic Factors on Age-Earnings Profiles,"
Journal of Human Resources (spring 1979).

————, and D. WISE, eds., *National Bureau of Economic Research Conference on Youth Unemployment*, 1979.

    BROWN, CHARLES, "Dead-End Jobs and Youth Unemployment";

    CLARK, KIM, and LAWRENCE SUMMERS, "The Dynamics of Youth Unem-
    ployment";

    CORCORAN, MARY, "Attitudes of Women and Changing Employment
    Patterns";

    ELLWOOD, DAVID, "Teenage Unemployment: Permanent Scar or Tem-
    porary Blemish";

    FREEMAN, RICHARD, and JAMES MEDOFF, "Why Does the Rate of Youth
    Labor Force Activity Differ Across Surveys?";

    HALL, ROBERT, "The Minimum Wage and Job Turnover in Markets for
    Youth Workers";

    LAYARD, RICHARD, "Youth Unemployment in Britain and the U.S. Com-
    pared";

    MINCER, JACOB, and LINDA LEIGHTON, "Turnover and Unemployment";

    REES, ALBERT, and WAYNE GRAY, "Family Effects in Youth Unemploy-
    ment";

WACHTER, MICHAEL, and CHONGSOO KIM, "Time Series Changes in Youth Joblessness";

WISE, DAVID, and ROBERT MEYER, "High School Preparation and Early Labor Market Experience."

GAVETT, THOMAS, et al., *Youth Unemployment and the Minimum Wage*, Bureau of Labor Statistics (Bulletin 165), 1970.

GRAMLICH, EDWARD M., "Impact of Minimum Wages on Other Wages, Employment, and Family Incomes," *Brookings Papers on Economic Activity* (2: 1976).

KALACHEK, EDWARD, "Determinants of Teen Age Employment," *The Journal of Human Resources* (winter 1969).

KATZ, ARNOLD, "Teenage Employment Effects of State Minimum Wages," *Journal of Human Resources* (spring 1973).

KING, ALLAN G., "Minimum Wages and the Secondary Labor Market," *Southern Economic Journal* (October 1974).

LEIGH, DUANE E., "The Occupational Mobility of Young Men, 1965–1970," *Industrial and Labor Relations Review* (October 1976).

LEVITAN, SAR A., "Coping with Teenage Unemployment," *The Teenage Unemployment Problem: What Are The Options?*, Congressional Budget Office (October 14, 1976).

LOVELL, MICHAEL C., "The Minimum Wage, Teenage Unemployment, and the Business Cycle," *Western Economic Journal* (December 1972).

MARSTON, STEPHEN, "Employment Instability and High Unemployment Rates," *Brookings Paper on Economic Activity* (1:1976).

MEYER, HERBERT E., "Jobs and Want Ads: A Look Behind the Words," *Fortune* (November 1978).

MINCER, JACOB, "Unemployment Effects of Minimum Wages," *Journal of Political Economy* (August 1972).

MOORE, THOMAS G., "The Effect of Minimum Wages on Teenage Unemployment Rates," *Journal of Political Economy* (July/August 1971).

NATIONAL CHILD LABOR COMMITTEE, *Rite of Passage: The Crisis of Youth's Transition from School to Work*. New York (1976).

RAGAN, JAMES J., JR., "Minimum Wages and the Youth Labor Market," *The Review of Economics and Statistics* (May 1977).

SILBERMAN, CHARLES, "What Hit the Teenagers," *Fortune* (April 1965).

SMITH, RALPH, "The Teenage Unemployment Problem: How Much Will Macro Policies Matter?", *The Teenage Unemployment Problem: What Are The Options?*, Congressional Budget Office (October 14, 1976).

WESTCOTT, D., "Youth in the Labor Force: An Area Study," *Monthly Labor Review* (July 1976).

WOLFBEIN, SEYMOUR L., ed., *Labor Market Information for Youths*. Philadelphia: Temple University School of Business Administration, 1975.

Michael L. Wachter

2

The Dimensions and Complexities of the Youth Unemployment Problem

Public policy discussion of the youth unemployment problem has focused on three developments. First, unemployment rates for youth are very high relative to those of adults. Second, over the past two decades, apart from cyclical fluctuations, youth unemployment rates have been increasing. This secular growth in teenage unemployment has meant an increase in the ratio of youth to non-youth unemployment rates and in particular of youth to prime age male unemployment rates. Third, black youth unemployment has grown relative to white youth unemployment.

This chapter will explore the dimensions of the youth unemployment problem. Clearly, youth unemployment is a major national problem. Less certain are its magnitude and distributional impact.

DR. MICHAEL WACHTER, *professor of economics at the University of Pennsylvania, is currently finishing a book on youth unemployment for the Twentieth Century Fund and has written numerous articles in this area. He is also a commissioner on the U.S. Minimum Wage Commission and is doing research under grants from the General Electric Foundation and the National Institutes of Child and Human Development.*

The official youth unemployment rate provides a useful and pessimistic assessment of the labor market status for that age group. Evaluating the policy information provided by the unemployment rate numbers, however, is a more complex undertaking than might initially appear to be the case. High or rising unemployment rates often, but not always, signal a policy problem.

The complications are numerous, but many relate to the fact that the concept of unemployment and the methodology for its measurement were originally intended mainly to assess trends in the performance of the economy. For example, prime age males tend to be in the labor force full time and have a strong attachment to their jobs. The ratio of those who are unemployed to those who are in the labor force—the unemployment rate—has an obvious and compelling meaning. Most of the time, however, the bulk of the youth population is neither employed nor unemployed. They are simply not in the labor market. Many are in school; others are in the military; and another group is involved in household activities such as child rearing. In addition, a disproportionate percentage of youth who are in the labor market are part-time workers. For these reasons, changes in the unemployment rate for youth can mean very different things.

This chapter is organized in the following fashion. The first section describes youth unemployment rates and why these rates are high relative to other age groups. The second analyzes cyclical factors in youth unemployment. It discusses why the youth unemployment problem is currently a structural rather than a cyclical problem. The third section provides further analysis of the structural issues and suggests alternative measures of youth unemployment and labor market status.

The High Unemployment Rates for Youth

THE YOUTH UNEMPLOYMENT RATE NUMBERS

To assess the youth unemployment problem, it is useful to begin by examining the pattern of the official Bureau of Labor Statistics (BLS) unemployment rate. The unemployment rate is defined as the number of unemployed divided by the number in the labor force. The BLS counts as unemployed all of those who are out of a job but are "actively seeking work." The labor force includes the unemployed and the employed.

That unemployment rates are relatively high for youth and especially high for black youth is shown in Table 1. Every youth age-sex group has a higher unemployment rate than the comparable nonyouth group or than the labor force as a whole (6 percent in 1978). As seen in Table 1, the lowest youth unemployment rate is 7.6 percent for white males twenty to twenty-four. Excluding the twenty to twenty-four age group, the lowest youth unemployment rate is 10.9 percent for white males eighteen to nineteen. Alternatively, the highest rate is for black females sixteen to seventeen and is above 40 percent. For the teenage group, unemployment rates range from two to seven times as high as the national average.

Within the youth groups, the data indicate a number of important differences. Perhaps most important is that black unemployment rates are considerably and consistently higher than white rates for every age and sex group. In each case, black youth unemployment rates are more than twice and occasionally three times as high as comparable white rates.

Contrary to the large race unemployment differentials, there are

TABLE 1. YOUTH UNEMPLOYMENT RATES, 1978

Age	Whites	
	Males	*Females*
16–17	16.9	17.1
18–19	10.8	12.4
20–24	7.6	8.3
25–54	3.0	4.9
Total 16+	4.5	6.2

Age	Blacks	
	Males	*Females*
16–17	40.0	41.7
18–19	30.8	36.5
20–24	20.0	21.3
25–54	6.6	8.7
Total 16+	10.9	13.1

Source: Employment and Earnings, Bureau of Labor Statistics, January 1979.

only minor differences in youth unemployment rates between sexes. However, female rates are always higher than male rates for the same age-race group. Yet the percentage unemployment differential between male and female youths is smaller than for prime age males and females.

Among youth categories, the younger the age group, the higher the unemployment rate. Among all race-sex groups, the sixteen to seventeen year olds in the labor force are twice as likely to be unemployed as the twenty to twenty-four year olds.

The trends in youth relative to nonyouth unemployment are shown in Table 2. Since year to year changes are a composite of long-run secular trends and short-run cyclical factors, it is important to disentangle the two. One method is to focus on those years when the prime age male unemployment rate was approximately equal to its 1978 value. For comparison purposes, 1955, 1964, 1972, and 1978 can be identified as equivalent years in terms of the degree of labor market tightness. Table 2 indicates a significant deterioration in the relative unemployment rates of youth relative to prime age males since 1955. The decline, however, took place between the mid 1950s through the early 1970s. By 1978, both the sixteen to nineteen and twenty to twenty-four age groups had improved their relative position somewhat in comparison with 1972. Although the

TABLE 2.   UNEMPLOYMENT RATE TRENDS, SELECTED YEARS 1955–1978

	1955	1964	1972	1978
Unemployment rates				
Both sexes, 16–19	11.0	16.2	16.2	16.3
Both sexes, 20–24	7.0	8.3	9.2	9.5
Males, 25–54	3.1	3.2	3.1	3.4
Unemployment ratios				
Both sexes, 16–19 / Males, 25–54	3.6	5.1	5.2	4.8
Both sexes, 20–24 / Males, 25–54	2.3	2.6	3.0	2.8

Sources: Employment and Earnings, Bureau of Labor Statistics, January 1979. *Economic Report of the President,* January 1979. Bureau of Labor Statistics, unpublished data.

situation has been improving, relative unemployment rates are still well above 1955 levels.

An additional finding is that black unemployment rates increase, relative to prime age males, over the entire 1955 to 1978 period. That is, the entire improvement in youth rates that has occurred over the past five years has been captured by white youth. This adds another dimension to the public concern about youth unemployment, namely, the widening of unemployment rates between white and black youths.

THE BASIS OF THE HIGH UNEMPLOYMENT RATES FOR YOUTH

Unemployment is a more complex phenomenon for youths than for other age groups. Traditionally, unemployment is divided into three categories: cyclical, frictional, and structural. For most age groups, especially prime age workers, the former two types dominate, and structural unemployment is not a major factor. For teenagers, all three are important; however, the structural component may be the most significant. Since the unemployment rate concept was designed to deal largely with frictional and cyclical unemployment, it is not specifically geared to the unique features of the youth market.

To illustrate these differences among age groups consider first the nature of prime age male unemployment. Except for major downturns in the economy, frictional unemployment may be the most important explanation as to why a prime age male worker would be out of a job. Indeed, when the economy is expanding and close to its peak level of production, the only prime age male workers who are unemployed are those who are between jobs. The jobs exist, and it is only a matter of weeks before those who are out of work accept another job. In addition, job mobility for this age group is often associated with an improvement in economic status. From a policy perspective, there is general agreement that frictional unemployment may actually contribute to the efficient workings of the economic system. Although it could be reduced by improving the flow of information about job vacancies and unemployed workers, frictional unemployment poses a small problem compared with cyclical and structural unemployment.

Cyclical unemployment is associated with recessions and periods when production is below capacity. During economic slumps, workers of all age groups are subject to layoffs. Since youths are a large percentage of the new entrants and reentrants into the labor market, they also suffer because new jobs are not being created fast enough to absorb them.

For prime age males, bouts of cyclical unemployment often mean being out of work, but awaiting recall from the same firm. These workers have accumulated the greatest seniority rights, and this guarantees they will be among the first who are returned to work when their employers' production schedules increase. They will remain in the labor force collecting unemployment compensation and/or other welfare benefits awaiting recall.

Cyclical or Keynesian unemployment is perhaps the easiest for government policy makers to deal with. It can be erased using expansionary monetary and fiscal policies. Tax cuts, new government expenditure programs, and "easy" money policies (that is, an increase in the rate of growth of the real money supply) have all been successful in lowering cyclical unemployment rates.

Youth unemployment, on the other hand, is much more difficult to classify. The key difference is that youth unemployment has structural, as well as frictional and cyclical, components. The structural problem is related to a broad range of factors. Perhaps most important are the relatively low skill and training levels of young people and the number of nonlabor market activities open to them. The low skill level of young workers is due to the inherent fact that few have been able to acquire specific or on-the-job training. In addition, many youth have not finished their general education. The sixteen to seventeen age group is either still in high school or just graduating. The eighteen to nineteen year olds are beginning either college or work careers. Only the twenty to twenty-four year olds may have both completed their schooling and acquired some initial specific job related training as well. This diversity among youth groups makes it impossible to generalize about the youth employment "problem." Rather, it is crucial to study separately the three relatively distinct age categories that span the youth population.

An additional factor contributing to the structural characteristics of the youth labor market is that there are many options open to youth that fit into traditional roles, besides entering the labor market. Young people may, for example, attend school, join the military, or remain at home and begin to raise their own families. In addition, they can combine these different activities; a disproportionate number of youth who are in the labor market are part-time workers. An increasing percentage of these individuals combines being full-time students and part-time workers.

Moreover, the choice of activities shifts frequently over the years. Relatively few young people age sixteen to nineteen work year-round, full-time. One traditional pattern for this group is to work full-time only during the summer months. Even for those who are not in school, changes in status between being employed, unemployed, and out of the labor force can occur several times over the year.

The low skill levels of young workers not only reduce the number of available jobs, but also mean that the job openings will often be in low-wage jobs. The presence of minimum wage laws may further reduce the demand for youth workers. However, the options of schooling, raising a family, etc., mean that there are significant alternatives to market work. Moreover, the income needs of youth can be satisfied, although often at a low level, by parental support and/or government social welfare programs such as food stamps, summer job programs, and, less frequently, public assistance. Hence, the unattractive "demand" situation for youth workers combines with the relatively attractive "supply" position created by these alternative activities and the availability of other sources of income to create a high level of unemployment.

There is an ongoing debate about whether unemployment among teenagers is a reflection of a job shortage or the desire of youth to pursue attractive nonwork activities. It might seem that if the BLS definition of unemployment is used, voluntary unemployment would be an unimportant element. If individuals are "actively seeking work," how can they be voluntarily out of work?

The answer is that individuals have a wage rate at which they are willing to work. They can be actively seeking work, but if the job with the minimum acceptable wage is not offered, they may remain unemployed. The BLS does not ask about the wage rate at which an individual is willing to work. In addition, as discussed below, the notion of "actively" seeking work is an ambiguous notion for many youth. This is particularly true for the very large group whose primary activity is schooling and which is interested in either part-time work during the school semester or summer work.

Given the data limitations, the job shortage versus supply question on teenage unemployment cannot be fully resolved. It is likely that both arguments are relevant. From a macroeconomic perspective, however, this debate misses a key question. *Even if there is a job shortage, however defined, can expansionary monetary and fiscal policies be used to increase the employment and decrease the unemployment rate of youth?* The next section focuses on this issue.

Cyclical Factors in Youth Unemployment

THE TRADE-OFF BETWEEN UNEMPLOYMENT AND INFLATION

The traditional view is that the cyclical factor in youth unemployment is always positive and large; that is, a job shortage for youth exists and can be solved using Keynesian monetary and fiscal policies. This type of thinking was incorporated, for example, in the Humphrey-Hawkins legislation. Although referring to a range of policy options, this bill, especially in earlier forms, sought a reduction in unemployment, and especially youth unemployment, largely through expansionary policies.

The Kennedy-Johnson tax cut and its initial success in lowering unemployment in the late 1960s led to this interpretation of youth unemployment. At the depths of the 1961 recession, the national unemployment rate was 6.7 percent while for teenagers, age sixteen to nineteen, it was 16.8 percent. After three years of recovery, through 1964, the aggregate rate had fallen to 5.2 percent while the teenage rate remained largely unchanged at 16.2 percent. In the early stages of the recovery, most of the gain from expansionary monetary and fiscal stimuli accrued to the adult unemployed. Thereafter, the trade-off shifted dramatically. As the national unemployment rate fell between 1965 and 1969 and labor markets tightened, more and more of the declining unemployment rate was captured by teenagers, minorities, and females. For example, between 1964 and 1969, the total unemployment rate fell an additional 1.7 points to 3.5 percent. At the same time, teenage unemployment declined a full 4 points to 12.2 percent.

The success of Keynesian demand policies in the late 1960s did not, however, go unquestioned. A dissenting view, identified primarily with Charles Killingsworth, argued that structural policies were actually responsible for lowering youth unemployment rates. He stressed, for example, the direct employment of youth in the Neighborhood Youth Corps (NYC), in the Manpower Development and Training Act (MDTA), and in the military during the high draft years of the Vietnam War. Those who believed that Keynesian policies were responsible for the decline in youth unemployment rates argued that the impact of the NYC programs was largely restricted to the summer months. In addition, both the NYC and the MDTA may have hired young people who were out of the labor force or employed in the private sector. That is, these programs may have increased employment in the government sector, but did not have much of an effect on the youth unemployment rates. In any case, the manpower programs during the 1960s were relatively small in scope.

Actually, the reduction in youth unemployment during the long expansion of the 1960s was not impressive when compared with the experience of the 1950s. For example, in the expansionary years of 1955–56, before public service employment was even on the policy agenda, teenage unemployment averaged 11 percent. Clearly, tight labor markets provide leverage to lower the unemployment rate of young workers.

This sensitivity of teenage unemployment rates to tight labor markets was highlighted by the recession of 1970. Between 1969 and 1970, while the national unemployment rate increased 1.4 percentage points, the teenage rate jumped 3 points back to 15.2 percent. Over the past decade, the teenage unemployment rate has not again declined to the 12.2 percent mark of 1969.

The use of expansionary monetary and fiscal policies to lower teenage unemployment rates when labor markets are already relatively tight, however, is not without cost. In particular, these periods of low unemployment are associated with higher or increasing rates of inflation.

In policy terms, an important question is whether the trade-off is simply between lower unemployment and a somewhat higher but stable inflation rate. If this is the cost, it may be inexpensive. To policy makers, the fact that (peacetime) periods of low teenage unemployment have only been achieved in the presence of highly expansionary monetary and fiscal policies is strong evidence in support of those policies. Indeed, it appears from a quick inspection of the data that only expansionary monetary and fiscal policies have succeeded in lowering youth unemployment rates to 10 percent. Certainly, nothing attempted during the 1970s has worked to reduce these rates to levels achieved in the mid-1950s and late 1960s.

Does this mean that Keynesian policies should be the accepted cure for youth unemployment? Since this cure does lower the youth unemployment rate, the only issue is the strength of the inflationary side effects from the treatment. Unfortunately, it appears that policies, sufficiently expansionary to lower unemployment rates, not only cause an increase in the inflation rate, but as long as unemployment remains low, cause *accelerating* inflation. Hence, the last few major expansions, 1966–69, 1971–73, and 1977–79, have all been associated with rapidly *rising rates of inflation*. This suggests a benchmark to be used to specify the dosage level of Keynesian policies the economy can absorb without developing the side effect of accelerating inflation.

EQUILIBRIUM UNEMPLOYMENT RATES

The equilibrium unemployment rate, or NAIRU (nonaccelerating-inflation rate of unemployment), is the benchmark which indicates the minimum unemployment rate which is compatible with a stable rate of inflation. When unemployment is below the equilibrium rate, inflation increases as firms bid wages higher to attract workers. When unemployment is above the equilibrium rate, the rate of inflation subsides. Given this definition, zero cyclical unemployment exists when the actual unemployment rate is equal to the equilibrium rate or NAIRU. Positive (negative) cyclical unemployment therefore exists when the unemployment rate is above (below) the equilibrium rate.

Most estimates of the current rate of equilibrium unemployment, including my own, range between 5.25 and 6.25 percent. Since the overall unemployment rate for the United States economy, at the beginning of 1979, was approximately 5.8 percent, the implication is that the cyclical unemployment rate was close to zero. This implies that the United States had fully recovered from the 1974–75 recession by the end of 1978. Indeed, the acceleration in the inflation rate during 1978 supports those who argue that the equilibrium unemployment rate is close to the upper end of the 5.25 to 6.25 percent range. This position has been adopted by the Joint Economic Committee in their 1979 report.

Disaggregating the unemployment rate confirms this picture of a near zero level of cyclical unemployment, even for youth. That is, for the economy of the U.S. in 1978, nonaccelerating inflation is compatible with a teenage unemployment rate of approximately 16 percent and a twenty to twenty-four year old unemployment rate of approximately 9 percent. My calculations of age specific equilibrium unemployment rates and the 1978 observed unemployment rates are shown in Table 3.

An equilibrium unemployment rate above 5 percent is a recent

TABLE 3.   ACTUAL AND EQUILIBRIUM UNEMPLOYMENT, 1978

Group	Actual Rate	Equilibrium Rate
Male		
16–17	19.2	18.1
18–19	13.2	13.1
20–24	9.1	7.9
25–34	4.3	3.6
35–44	2.8	2.5
45–54	2.8	2.5
55–64	2.7	2.8
65+	4.2	3.6
Female		
16–17	19.5	18.7
18–19	15.3	15.7
20–24	10.1	9.1
25–34	6.7	6.3
35–44	5.0	4.7
45–54	4.0	3.7
55–64	3.2	3.1
65+	3.8	3.5
Total 16+	6.0	5.6

The method for calculating the Equilibrium Rates is presented in Michael L. Wachter, "The Changing Cyclical Responsiveness of Wage Inflation over the Postwar Period," *Brookings Papers on Economic Activity* (1:1976).

development. To most economists, 1955–56 was a period when there was virtually no cyclical unemployment. The 4.25 observed unemployment rate of that period was entirely frictional and structural in nature; that is, the equilibrium rate was also 4.25 percent. Most of the increase in the equilibrium unemployment rate since 1955 is due to the demographic compositional shift toward younger and female workers. As a direct consequence of the baby boom of the late 1950s, young workers, both male and female, have been increasing as a percentage of the labor force. For young male workers, labor force participation rates have increased somewhat, so that the increase in their relative population size translates directly into an increase in their relative percentage in the labor force. For females, aged sixteen to thirty-four, rapidly increasing participation rates have swelled the population growth into a dramatic increase in labor force growth. Whereas workers aged sixteen to twenty-four were 16.7 percent of the labor force in 1960, they constituted 25 percent by 1978. Since youth have higher unemployment rates than nonyouth, an increase in the percentage of sixteen to twenty-four year olds will cause the national unemployment rate to increase. This can occur even if the unemployment rates for each age-sex group remain unchanged. I estimate that, of the increase in the equilibrium unemployment rate over the past two decades, a full percentage point is due simply to the changing composition of the labor force.

INCREASING YOUTH UNEMPLOYMENT

If cyclical unemployment is not a factor, what can explain the increase in relative youth unemployment between 1955 and 1979? My explanation for this phenomenon is an increase in the equilibrium unemployment for youth due to "cohort overcrowding." A large increase in the flow of young workers into a competitive labor market need not create a structural unemployment problem. U.S. labor markets, especially for individuals at the bottom rung of the skill ladder, have institutional features which encourage youth unemployment. Often mentioned as causal factors are high income and government programs such as the minimum wage and public assistance.

Government labor market programs have changed dramatically

since the 1960s. This country, for example, virtually did not have an operational minimum wage policy between 1947 and 1967. Minimum wages were set at a constant ratio to wages paid elsewhere in the economy. The major industries which hired numerous workers at low wages could obtain an exemption from the minimum wage laws by arguing before Congress that if they were forced to pay the minimum wage, significant unemployment would result. The outcome was a policy that exempted most of those workers and industries which might have been affected.

By 1967, the influx of young workers threatened the employment and relative wage status of the older workers in the low-paying secondary markets. Congress responded by extending minimum wage coverage to those labor markets. The minimum wage coverage in 1967 jumped from 39.9 percent to 53.4 percent of civilian employment, and that jump largely extended coverage to low-wage workers. There had been some minor increases in coverage before 1967, but increases in the coverage rate only have an impact when they affect the workers who are actually earning the minimum wage. Throughout the postwar period, the most significant change in minimum wage coverage was the increase in 1967.

At the same time, Congress increased welfare payments. In the 1960s, Aid to Families with Dependent Children (AFDC) payments grew relative to the market wage. The biggest rise in welfare payments was "in-kind transfers" such as the Food Stamp Program. The mechanism through which welfare payments can alter the income available to young people depends upon their family status. Where the young people have already established their own family unit, they would be eligible directly for welfare payments if their income were low. But in most cases, especially for teenagers, the youths are still living at home and thus are not eligible themselves for benefits. When the youths are working while living at home, they increase the family income and thus can affect their parents' eligibility.

It is the simultaneous occurrence of the baby boom and the entire set of changes in government policies that is central to explaining the increase in the relative unemployment of sixteen to twenty-four year olds. The entrance of the baby boom children into the labor market resulted in much lower wages for young people relative to other workers with established careers. As the relative wages for youth declined, the minimum wage which was first being applied to the service and retail trades sectors became more relevant. In addition, the cost of being unemployed declined as welfare levels increased faster and youth market wages slower than the general wage level. Finally, rising family income, especially for the nonpoor, provided an alternative to regular market work and the opportunity to explore market jobs and new market opportunities.

THE UNEMPLOYMENT POOL AT ZERO CYCLICAL UNEMPLOYMENT

Evidence that the economy is currently close to a zero level of cyclical unemployment can be seen by examining the characteristics of the unemployment pool in 1978. What emerges is a picture of imbalance, with the unemployed largely being the young and the unskilled; approximately 50 percent of the total unemployment is accounted for by workers in the sixteen to twenty-four age group. Table 4 shows that unemployment rates are highest among lower-skilled workers. Specifically, it indicates the mismatch between the employment and unemployment pools when the economy is at the

TABLE 4.   OCCUPATIONAL EMPLOYMENT AND UNEMPLOYMENT POOLS, 1978

Occupation	Percent Unemployed	Percent Employed
Professional and Technical	7.4	15.1
Managers and Administrators, except Farmers	4.1	10.7
Sales Workers	4.9	6.3
Clerical Workers	16.7	17.9
Craft and Kindred Workers	11.6	13.1
Operatives, except Transport	18.5	11.5
Transport Equipment Operatives	3.8	3.8
Nonfarm Laborers	10.9	5.0
Service Workers	19.9	13.6
Farm Workers	2.1	3.0
TOTAL	100.0	100.0

Source: Employment and Earnings, January 1979, Household Data Annual Averages.

TABLE 5. UNEMPLOYED PERSONS BY REASON FOR UNEMPLOYMENT, 1978

Reason for Unemployment	Persons, 16 and Over Percent Unemployment Pool	Persons, 16–19 Percent Unemployment Pool
On layoff	11.5	4.1
Other job losers	30.0	14.9
Job leavers	14.1	10.5
Reentrants	30.0	28.8
New entrants	14.3	41.8
TOTAL	100.0	100.0

Source: Employment and Earnings, January 1978, Household Data Annual Averages.

equilibrium rate. Three of the lowest skilled occupational categories (service workers, nonfarm laborers, and operatives) account for 50 percent of the unemployment. On the other hand, these three categories include only 30 percent of the employment pool. Table 5 indicates that layoffs, the cause of unemployment typically associated with recessions and inadequate demand, accounted for only 11.5 percent of the unemployment pool. Unemployment spells initiated by actions of the workers (quits, reentrants, and new entrants) accounted for almost 60 percent of the total unemployment. For teenagers, only 4.1 percent of the unemployed are on layoff status, and 80 percent were either reentrants, new entrants, or job leavers.

To summarize, when the economy is close to its equilibrium level of 5.5 to 6 percent, the unemployment pool has a number of important characteristics. The great bulk of the unemployed are young workers sixteen to twenty-four and workers with low skill levels. Only a small minority of workers are on layoff status, which is the type of unemployment normally associated with cyclical fluctuations. Finally, there are few prime age skilled workers in the unemployment pool.

The equilibrium unemployment rate is constructed for the sole purpose of defining the noninflationary limits of general aggregate demand policies. As a result, it should be differentiated from the usual meaning attached to the full-employment, unemployment rate. That rate, as it is often used in the political process, tends to be identified with a socially optimal rate that could be achieved using a broad range of policy tools. Suppose, for example, that the economy is currently at the NAIRU, but policy makers would like to achieve still lower unemployment for the overall economy or the youth groups in particular. This might be achieved using structural policies such as manpower training, employment tax credits, and/or a youth subminimum wage. Over the long run these policies can lower the equilibrium rate or NAIRU. In the short run, to avoid accelerating inflation, any economic stimulus resulting from such policies would have to be offset by decreasing other government expenditure programs.

Alternative Methods for Measuring the Labor Market Status of Youth

The previous section discussed the cyclical aspects of youth unemployment. The data suggested that, as of 1978–79, the youth unemployment rates were dominated by structural factors. This large structural component is due to several features of the youth labor market: the low skill levels associated with most youth jobs, the availability of alternatives to market work, such as schooling, and the prevalence of part-time and part-of-the-year working patterns.

Complicating an evaluation of the youth unemployment issue is that, from society's perspective, working year-round, full-time is not necessarily the most desirable activity for a young person. For prime age males, the social ordering of activities is clear; working year-round, full-time is the desired role. For young people, particularly for teenagers, being in school may be preferable, from society's perspective, to working. To some, military service also ranks above civilian employment. For young females, child rearing may be more favorable than working.

In evaluating the official youth unemployment rate statistics, these problems suggest that alternative labor market measures be constructed. In this section, alternative unemployment rates, a joblessness measure, and employment to population ratios are explored. The objective is to provide different and complementary perspectives on the structural nature of the youth unemployment problem.

ALTERNATIVE UNEMPLOYMENT RATE MEASURES

One obvious change from the usual unemployment rate is to include the military as part of the labor force. Indeed, the BLS differentiates between the civilian and total labor force by including the military in the latter definition. For the overall economy, including the military as employed has little effect since it is a small "industry." For youth, however, the military is a very large employer. Substituting the total for the civilian labor force as the denominator of the unemployment rate has the effect of lowering the unemployment rate statistics. (The number who are unemployed, of course, remains the same.)

A second change, which would broaden the denominator of the unemployment rate still further, would be to add those who are in school to those who are in the total labor market. A problem with analyzing the policy significance of youth unemployment rates is that being in the labor market may be inferior, in the long run, to being in school. The importance of schooling for lifetime economic status creates the potential that changes in youth unemployment rates will not accurately signal changes in their economic position.

Take the case of an increase in school enrollment for sixteen to seventeen year olds caused by a reduction in the high school dropout rate. If these individuals were for the most part employed, the unemployment rate will increase as the dropouts return to school. The unemployment rate may actually increase further if these dropouts now decide to work part-time to finance their full-time schooling. Since people who want to work part-time are frequently changing jobs, they tend to have a high incidence of unemployment.

Increased schooling means a more skilled and flexible work force. A higher skill level translates into a lower incidence of unemployment during the adult years, a higher level of family income, and a lower probability of being on welfare. The lifetime economic status of youth is improving as their unemployment rate increases.

The newly constructed unemployment rate is denoted U2. The numerator remains the number of unemployed (U). The denominator is now the labor force (L), plus the military in that age group (M), plus those in school (S). To avoid double counting, one must then subtract those who are simultaneously in school and in the labor force and consequently would be counted in both S and L. The resulting unemployment rates are shown in Column 2 of Table 6.

The new unemployment rates present a very different picture from the official BLS unemployment rates (Column 1). First, the new rates are much lower than traditional youth unemployment

TABLE 6. ALTERNATIVE MEASURES OF UNEMPLOYMENT

	U1 or BLS Unemployment Rate [1]	*U2 or Unemployment Divided by Labor Force + School + Military* [2]	*U3 or Unemployment of Nonenrollees Divided by Labor Force + School + Military* [3]
Males, White			
16–17	17.1	10.1	4.8
18–19	10.9	8.0	6.1
20–24	7.6	6.4	5.8
Males, Black			
16–17	40.7	15.4	7.8
18–19	30.9	18.5	14.2
20–24	20.1	15.2	13.6
Females, White			
16–17	17.1	9.8	4.8
18–19	12.3	9.5	7.6
20–24	8.3	7.5	6.9
Females, Black			
16–17	41.9	14.8	8.7
18–19	36.8	23.8	18.4
20–24	21.6	18.6	16.8

[1] See Table 1.

[2] Measured as $\dfrac{U}{L + M + S - (S\eta L)}$ where U is the number of unemployed, L is the civilian labor force, M is the number in the military, S is the number in school, and $(S\eta L)$ indicates those who are both in school and in the civilian labor force.

[3] Measured as $\dfrac{U - (U\eta S)}{L + M + S - (S\eta L)}$.

rates. Second, there is no longer a monotonic decline in the unemployment rates with age. Since a greater proportion of sixteen to seventeen year olds go to school than other groups, the decline in their unemployment rates, when comparing U2 with U, is the largest. Third, black U2 remains considerably higher than white U2 rates for comparable age-sex groups.

If schooling as an activity is to be treated symmetrically with market work, one further adjustment must be made to the unemployment rate. In the BLS calculations, an individual cannot be counted both as employed and unemployed at the same time. This is not a facetious distinction. Workers, specifically those who want to moonlight and work at more than one job, can be both employed at the first job and unemployed while looking for the second job. According to the definition of unemployment, however, such a worker is counted as employed. The same issue arises when schooling is included. If individuals are in school, should they also be counted as unemployed if they are looking for a job as well? The U2 measure does count them as unemployed. It is useful, however, to establish a U3 measure which excludes this group from the unemployment pool. The justification for this is that individuals whose major activity is school are likely to be part-time workers with a relatively marginal attachment to a job. The fact that they are in school indicates that they will soon be looking for a different kind of job. These individuals tend to have a high incidence of unemployment.

Whether or not one agrees with this argument, U3 is still an interesting measure of unemployment. Correctly interpreted, it is the unemployment rate of nonenrolled youth as a percentage of the population that is in school, the military, or the labor force. This measure highlights an obvious problem group in the labor force. A frequent argument is that youth unemployment is not a serious issue since many of the unemployed are part-timers helping to put themselves through school. To the extent that they can remain in school, short-run bouts of unemployment are not a cause of great concern. On the other hand, the nonschoolers who are also looking but cannot find a job are much more likely to be individuals that pose a social policy problem. The U3 unemployment rates, depicted in Column 3 of Table 6, isolate this group.

The differences between U1 and U3 are even larger than for U1 and U2. First, the unemployment rates are again reduced considerably, with the largest reductions affecting the youngest age group. For example, for white youth sixteen to seventeen, the unemployment rate for nonenrollees, as a percentage of those in school and in the total labor force, is 4 percent. This shows clearly the extent to which sixteen to seventeen year olds are really a distinct group from eighteen to nineteen and twenty to twenty-four year olds. The great bulk of these individuals is still in school, and very few have neither a job nor a school to attend. If schooling is viewed as a job (an investment in human capital for future productivity), then this age group is nearly fully employed.

The school enrollment rate for white males sixteen to nineteen, as an annual average, was 63.3 percent in 1978. It is useful, however, to analyze the data for the nonsummer months as well as the annual averages. For example, during the first quarter of 1978, the school enrollment rate for white males sixteen to nineteen was 80.9 percent. The U3 rate in the first quarter of 1978 was 2.6 percent. That is, most of the sixteen to seventeen year olds are in school in the winter, and many of these are unemployed during the summer. The unemployment rate for white male nonenrollees, sixteen to seventeen, during the winter is below the unemployment rate for white, prime age males.

Even for blacks, age sixteen to seventeen, unemployment while not in school is concentrated in the summer months. For black males, age sixteen to seventeen, U3 is only 7.8 percent compared with a BLS measured unemployment rate of 40.7. Looking at the first quarter of 1978, instead of the annual data, the U3 rate falls to 4 percent.

The U3 measure almost reverses the picture that unemployment is highest for the youngest of the youth group and lowest for the oldest. As shown in Table 6, unemployment rates for sixteen to seventeen year olds are the lowest. But eighteen to nineteen year olds still have slightly higher U3 rates than the twenty to twenty-four year olds. This, however, is changed if the first quarter data are used. Unemployment for the nonschool population is highest for the twenty to twenty-four age group. In any case, the unemployment rates are all quite close to prime age male unemployment according to the BLS definition.

An important result of Table 6 is to show that black unemployment for the eighteen to twenty-four age group remains a problem even after moving from the U2 to the U3 measure. Having narrowed the definition so that it only covers the nonenrolled as a percentage of the school and work forces, it is disturbing that the resulting U3 measure is still approximately 15 percent for nonwhites. Moreover, the black U3 rates for the eighteen to twenty-four age group are still more than double the white U3 rates for comparable groups.

There are important limitations to the U2 and U3 measures. If labor market conditions are adverse, some youth who would prefer to work may decide to remain in school. Although it would be helpful if attending school automatically translated into increased training, this is obviously not the case. Since it is not possible to measure those youth who are pushed into school and are not learning, U2 and U3 may understate the youth unemployment problem. All the various unemployment statistics have their benefits and weaknesses. It is for this reason that they are best used together to provide different perspectives on the issue.

"JOBLESSNESS" AND THE "RESIDUAL RATE"

Given the focus on the alternative activities open to youth, an important group, from a policy perspective, is the group reported as being not in the labor force, not in school, and not in the military. The key question is what are the individuals in this group doing.

One group in this category is likely to contain the most disadvantaged and/or unskilled individuals in society. They may be high school dropouts who also cannot find a job or, at least, cannot find a job that pays more than the minimum wage. They may be youths from a welfare family who, if they accept a job, would cost their families their eligibility. They might be individuals who are in poor health and, for this reason, cannot work or go to school.

Alternatively, this group also contains individuals who are doing quite well. For example, it includes females who are beginning to raise a family and students who may take the summer off and hence get factored into the annual data. Table 7 provides the "residual rate," that is, the percentage of the population that is not in the labor force, military, or school.

Table 7. Unemployment Rate and the Percentage that Is Neither
in School Nor in the Total Labor Force

	BLS [1] Unemployment Rate, U/L	"Residual Rate" [2] (Nonlabor Force, Nonschool, Nonmilitary,) Divided by the Age-Race-Sex Specific Population
Male, White		
16–17	17.1	8.2
18–19	10.9	4.5
20–24	7.6	3.3
Male, Black		
16–17	40.7	11.7
18–19	30.9	10.4
20–24	20.1	9.2
Female, White		
16–17	17.1	13.6
18–19	12.3	16.1
20–24	8.3	23.6
Female, Black		
16–17	41.9	16.6
18–19	36.8	24.9
20–24	21.6	27.6

[1] Same as Table 5, column 1.

[2] Measured by Pn/P where Pn is the number who are not in school, not in the military. P is the number in the population. Alternative measure is:

$$\frac{P - L - M - S + (S\eta L)}{P}$$

The data isolate the following patterns. First, the female rate is much higher than the male rate for each age group. A good part of that difference, given similarities in their unemployment rates, is likely to be due to factors such as family responsibilities. To argue that the difference in the "residual rate" is due to discouragement, etc., would seem to require that the unemployment rates were relatively high for that particular age-sex group. Second, the "residual rate" decreases with age for males and decreases with age for females. This also supports the notion that seasonal schooling for males and childbearing for females are important factors in determining who falls into this residual group.

The disturbing statistics are for blacks; their residual as well as their unemployment rates are high. This is particularly true for black males in the youth group. The "residual rate" for black females is always higher than the white female rate, perhaps indicating a policy problem, but the increase in that rate between sixteen to seventeen year olds and twenty to twenty-four year olds is proportional to the increase in white rates for those age groups. Certainly, the increase with age is due, at least in part, to the fact that fertility rates increase between ages sixteen and twenty-four. Indeed, it is possible to argue that even the difference in residual rates between white and black females for each age group may reflect differential levels of fertility.

For black males the results are more discouraging. Whereas the white "residual rate" declines from 8.2 to 3.3 percent between sixteen to seventeen and twenty to twenty-four year olds, the black "residual rate" only drops from 11.7 to 9.2 percent. Given the lower income for blacks relative to whites, it is less likely that more of the blacks are not working or in school because of positive social and economic factors.

When added to the unemployment rate, one potential use of the "residual rate" is to develop a modified "joblessness index." The term "modified" is used because if the traditional usage of joblessness were adopted, those in school and not employed would also be included. I prefer to exclude this group because schooling for them may be a preferred status to employment. For example, adding college students together with high school dropouts who are unemployed is not useful in clarifying the economic status of youth. Indeed, it would also be preferable not to add together the unemployment rate with the "residual category." The reason is due to the numerous explanations for not working or being in school. Given present data there is simply no reliable way of determining the percentage of this group that is policy relevant. As a start, it would be desirable to be able to classify youth who have access to relatively high sources of income.

It is important to recognize that many of those who might be classified as being part of the "disadvantaged residual rate" do not necessarily form a pool of discouraged workers ready to accept a job if one were available. There is evidence that jobs exist for the unskilled when the economy is at the equilibrium unemployment rate. The problems are that those jobs are not attractive given the availability of other sources of income, ranging from family income to government transfer programs to illegal activities. In addition, many in this category may have low skill levels, compounded by low job attachment. Thus, the problem for many unemployed workers and disadvantaged nonparticipants, when the economy is at the equilibrium rate, is low skills and hence low wage levels in the context of today's social welfare programs and high standards of family income.

EMPLOYMENT/POPULATION RATIOS

In the previous section, a joblessness index was created by adding the "residual rate" (that is, nonparticipants and nonschool enrollees) to the unemployed rates. An alternative approach is illustrated by the employment/population ratio (including the military in both employment and population). This still gives only a partial picture since it omits those who are in school. The rates for both 1965 and 1978, two years when the national unemployment rate was close to the equilibrium unemployment rate, are shown in Table 8.

There are several advantages of the employment/population ratio as a measure of joblessness. First, it avoids having to decide what percentage of the "residual rate" (Pn of Table 7) should be added to the unemployment rate. Any concept that builds upon the unemployment rate has the danger of being confused with a notion of an augmented unemployment rate or as an unemployment plus hardship index. Since many of those who do not have jobs either because they are in school or involved in some household activity are not discouraged, disadvantaged, or dissatisfied, it is not useful to interpret joblessness as defining the boundaries of a population that needs remedial policy action. The employment ratio has a clearer meaning; it is simply those who are working as a percentage of the population.

There is still a problem in that some tend to view an increase in E/P as indicating an improvement in a group's labor market status.

TABLE 8.   EMPLOYMENT/POPULATION RATIOS, 1965 & 1978 *

	1965	*1978*
Males, White		
16–17	38.9	46.3
18–19	63.5	69.2
20–24	83.4	82.0
Males, Black		
16–17	29.0	20.5
18–19	56.9	46.6
20–24	83.4	66.3
Females, White		
16–17	24.5	40.7
18–19	43.8	56.8
20–24	46.2	63.8
Females, Black		
16–17	12.6	16.0
18–19	28.9	31.4
20–24	47.7	49.8

* Includes military for each age, sex, race group in both numerator and denominator of employment/population ratio.

As stressed above, to the extent that E/P increases because S/P falls, the affected group may be doing worse, not better. Schooling is not only a form of investment in human capital, but also a form of consumption, undertaken particularly by youth from families with a very high income. An improvement in the long-term outlook for the youth group, in absolute terms and/or relative to older cohorts, is likely to lead to an increase in schooling. In addition, an increase in E/P generated by more students working part-time to finance their education cannot be viewed as a welfare improvement. Although financing one's education may be good for the psyche, that view is held more by parents for their offspring than by the offspring themselves. It is unlikely that the large increase in students working part-time is a reflection of a shift in preferences toward viewing hard work as a virtue. Rather, as the baby boom parents now find that educating three children is costly and a potential threat to their retirement savings, they are more likely to request that the offspring work so as to reduce parental expenses.

The results in Table 8 contrast sharply with the picture of increasing youth unemployment. With the exception of black males, youth employment has grown even faster than their rapidly growing population. The largest gains in E/P have been for white females. These developments in youth employment indicate that the economy is creating a considerable number of jobs for youths.

For black males, sixteen to twenty-four, however, the problem of increasing unemployment is compounded by declining E/P. Although employment for black males sixteen to twenty-four is growing, it is not growing nearly as fast as its population.

The declining E/P for black males, sixteen to twenty-four, combined with the deterioration in the unemployment rates of black relative to white youth indicate that the youth labor market problem is concentrated among blacks. Understanding the dimensions of this problem, however, is complicated by the improvement in relative earnings and school enrollment for black youth.

Although the employment situation has worsened for blacks relative to whites, the relative wages for blacks have increased continuously during the last decade. The usual full-time weekly earnings of youth whose major activities are other than school also show a similar pattern. Here again, the gap between black and white wage differentials has narrowed over time. Except for females aged sixteen to seventeen, the wage of all black groups rose more than that of the comparable white groups. A puzzling question is why the black male groups, whose labor market condition measured by unemployment-employment indicators was worse than any other group, enjoyed relatively better earnings growth than other groups.

In addition to the relative wage trends, school enrollment rates have also increased substantially more for black youth than for white youth. Indeed, except for females age twenty to twenty-four, the enrollment rates for white youths decreased for all age-sex groups between 1965 and 1978. During the same period, the enrollment rates for blacks consistently increased. Furthermore, although the enrollment rates for all black age-sex groups were lower than those for the corresponding white groups in 1965, the situation was reversed by 1978. That is, by 1978, the enrollment rates for all black age-sex groups were higher than for the comparable white groups.

Does the increase in school enrollment rates for black males equal the decline in their E/P rates? The increase in school enrollment captures almost all of the decline in E/P for black males sixteen to seventeen. For black males eighteen to nineteen, it picks up four of the ten percentage point decline. For the twenty to twenty-four black male group, a seventeen percentage point decline on E/P is reduced to ten percentage points when S/P is added.

Table 9 shows the percentage of youth employed or in school (or both) in 1965 and 1978. Among all age-sex youth groups, whites have a higher ratio of employment plus schooling than blacks. The trend, however, is less obvious. The increase in white employment ratios is, in part, due to their declining school enrollment and increasing part-time work while in school. The decrease in black employment ratios, is, in part, due to their increasing school enrollments. In addition, black enrollment has gained without a significant increase in after-school work (comparable to that found for white enrollees).

TABLE 9. EMPLOYMENT + SCHOOL POPULATION, 1965 & 1978

	1965	*1978*
Male, White		
16–17	88.0	87.6
18–19	91.0	90.0
20–24	94.0	91.1
Male, Black		
16–17	83.2	82.0
18–19	83.0	77.0
20–24	88.9	78.5
Female, White		
16–17	80.0	83.1
18–19	71.0	77.6
20–24	52.7	71.2
Female, Black		
16–17	74.0	77.0
18–19	56.9	61.4
20–24	52.5	59.5

Conclusions

The youth labor market over the past two decades has been characterized by very high and secularly increasing relative unemployment rates. In addition, within the youth group, unemployment rates for blacks have increased relative to the unemployment rates for whites.

These developments are usually attributed to a combination of cyclical and structural factors. The argument developed in this chapter stresses the structural characteristics of the youth labor market. First, during 1978 and 1979, the unemployment rate was close to its equilibrium level. The equilibrium unemployment rate defines the minimum rate that can be achieved by monetary and fiscal policies, without accelerating inflation. When the economy is at its equilibrium level, there is zero cyclical unemployment. In this framework, there is not a shortage of jobs for youth; that is, creating additional jobs using traditional Keynesian tools would lead to accelerating inflation. Second, the increase in unemployment rates for youth over the past two decades has been due to increases in the equilibrium rates. An explanation for this development is the effect of the baby boom and recent changes in government social welfare and labor market programs.

This does not mean that society should be satisfied with current levels of youth unemployment. The equilibrium rate should be differentiated from the usual meaning attached to the full-employment, unemployment rate. The latter rate, as it is often used in the political process, tends to be identified with a socially optimal rate that can be achieved using a broad range of policy tools. Structural policies, such as manpower training and employment tax credits have been suggested as methods for reducing the equilibrium rate of youth unemployment.

The ongoing structural problems in the youth labor market are due to a large number of factors. They include the low-skill and hence low-wage levels associated with most youth jobs, the availability of alternatives to market work (such as schooling), and the prevalence of part-time work attachments. Complicating an evaluation of the structural issues is that, for young people, attending school may be preferable to working full-time, year-round. Given these complexities, the traditional BLS unemployment rate tells only part of the story. In order to develop a more complete picture, it is desirable to analyze alternative measures of labor market conditions. These include joblessness indices and employment to population ratios.

For most teenage youth, schooling is their major activity. Youth unemployment during the school year, as a percentage of the youth population (as distinguished from the labor force) is considerably below official unemployment rates. For many youth, high unemployment rates are due to the attractive nonwork options available to them. These individuals will develop firm work attachments when they are ready for a steady career. In addition, at least for white youth, unemployment rates have been declining relative to the rates for older workers since 1972.

An analysis of the full range of statistics indicates that the youth unemployment problem is concentrated among black youth. For black youth, and especially black males, the unemployment problem continues to worsen. The extent of this problem, however, is difficult to assess. The declining employment to population ratios and increasing unemployment rates have taken place in a period of rising black youth school enrollment rates and increasing relative wages for black youth. These developments may suggest that, within the black youth group, there is an increasing dispersion of labor market opportunities and performance.

Given relatively low skills and specific training, the high youth unemployment rates do not mean a large output loss to society. That is, if all of the youth who wanted to work were to be given jobs, the resulting increase in output would be relatively small. For the youth themselves, however, unemployment may have very significant economic costs.

As today's youth age, the great majority of them will move on to stable, higher paying jobs. For a minority of youths, however, high unemployment and poor school performance will translate into ongoing economic problems. As these individuals age, their unemployment rates will decline substantially; yet their economic problems will remain. The manifestation of these problems will be low-wage workers and low-income families.

Bibliography

ADAMS, ARVIL V., and GARTH MANGUM, *The Lingering Crisis of Youth Unemployment.* Kalamazoo, Mich.: W. E. Upjohn Institute, 1978.

CLARK, KIM, and LAWRENCE SUMMERS, "Labor Market Dynamics and Unemployment: A Reconsideration," *Brookings Papers on Economic Activity* (1: 1979).

DOERINGER, PETER B., and MICHAEL PIORE, *Internal Labor Markets and Manpower Analysis.* Lexington, Mass.: D. C. Heath, 1971.

EASTERLIN, RICHARD A., *Population, Labor Force and Long Swings in Economic Growth: The American Experience.* New York: Columbia University Press, 1968.

EHRENBERG, RONALD G., "The Demographic Structure of Unemployment Rates and Labor Market Transition Probabilities," paper prepared for the National Commission for Manpower Policy, 1979.

FREEMAN, RICHARD B., *The Overeducated American.* New York: Academic Press, 1976.

KALACHEK, EDWARD, "Determinants of Teen Age Unemployment," *The Journal of Human Resources* (winter 1969).

KILLINGSWORTH, CHARLES C., "The Fall & Rise of the Idea of Structural Unemployment," Proceedings of the Thirty-first Annual Meeting of the Industrial Relations Research Association (August 1978).

LEVITAN, SAR A., and ROBERT TAGGART, III, *Employment and Earnings Inadequacy: A New Social Indicator.* Baltimore: Johns Hopkins Press, 1974.

NATIONAL COMMISSION FOR MANPOWER POLICY, *From School to Work: Improving the Transition.* Washington, D.C., 1976.

PERRY, CHARLES R., et al., *The Impact of Government Manpower Programs.* Philadelphia: Industrial Relations Unit, University of Pennsylvania, 1975.

REUBENS, BEATRICE G., *The Measurement and Interpretation of Teenage Unemployment in the United States and Other Countries.* Washington, D.C.: U.S. Dept. of Labor, February 1978.

WACHTER, MICHAEL L., "The Changing Cyclical Responsiveness of Wage Inflation Over the Postwar Period," *Brookings Papers on Economic Activity* (1: 1976).

————, "The Demographic Impact on Unemployment: Past Experience and the Outlook for the Future," *Demographic Trends and Full Employment,* National Commission for Manpower Policy, Special Report No. 12 (December 1976).

————, "Intermediate Swings in Labor-Force Participation," *Brookings Papers on Economic Activity* (2: 1977).

Elijah Anderson

3

Some Observations
of Black Youth Employment

Black inner city youth unemployment constitutes an intractable social problem for the nation as a whole and for local urban areas in particular, tearing at the social and moral fabric of the society in which we all live. The problem expresses itself among youth in the form of low self-esteem, alienation, crime, and other anti-social behavior.

While the problem is difficult and implicates various sectors of the society, relatively little is known, and even less understood, concerning black youth unemployment. The available literature tends to focus on the statistics or on the "structural" aspects of the problem; the value of such perspectives cannot be denied. But very little attention has been given to the perspectives of the unemployed youth themselves.

Thus, in gathering materials for this chapter, I walked the streets of Philadelphia and conducted in-depth interviews with numerous

DR. ELIJAH ANDERSON *is assistant professor of sociology and education at the University of Pennsylvania where he is a fellow at the Center for Urban Ethnography. He has written the book* A Place on the Corner: Rank and Identity of Black Street Corner Men.

inner city black male youths. Usually over coffee at a conveniently situated coffee shop or restaurant in the city, I spoke with them about their jobs, their job prospects, family backgrounds, educational backgrounds, their general life situations. I also spoke with some of those, both blacks and whites, who employ such youth. My purpose was to gain a picture of the work and the "street" situation as people experience and view them. What emerges, then, is a necessarily "unsystematic" sample of the youth and their attitudes about work and their involvements with it. It was from this set of ethnographic experiences that the following suggestive essay was generated, with the hope of conveying some insight and understanding of the condition of unemployed and employed black youth of the urban environment.

Over the past two decades, American society has undergone important social change in the area of race relations. The change is most striking, perhaps, with regard to the generally perceived "place" of blacks, from the point of view of blacks themselves and from the point of view of others, especially those who sense themselves to be in competition with blacks for jobs and for other privileges. Yet, particularly among black inner city youth, there continues to exist a large amount of frustration and impatience with the rate of black inclusion into the American occupational structure.

Inspired by the Civil Rights movement, which culminated in the assassination of the Reverend Martin Luther King, Jr., the urban riots of the 1960s, and subsequent affirmative action programs, black identity and self-concept have undergone significant revision, particularly among the young. It appears that the militancy of the 1960s has given way to a new sense of racial pride and self-assertiveness that has been slowly diffusing through urban black communities. With raised consciousness, the young, unskilled black worker often perceives himself useful only to the most exploitative employer, in the most menial of jobs, and then receives little or no job security, advancement, benefits, and at times no pay. With the increased emphasis on self, young blacks are tending to be more selective about the jobs they will perform, and often will not accept employment and work conditions they consider to be demeaning. This attitude appears in striking contrast to that of an earlier generation of blacks, many of whom accepted almost any available work. The youth tend to feel they are entitled to and deserve "much better jobs" than they are presently able to obtain.

As the black self-concept has undergone this revision, the media have focused much attention on black youth, especially black males. Young blacks are very often portrayed as angry, militant, insolent, violent, and fearsome. As middle-class professionals, black and white, flock back to refurbish and reinhabit the inner city, they often find themselves living close-by black ghetto areas, sharing the streets and supermarkets with these young "tough-looking" black males. At night they watch television news and learn that it was a young black male who committed the stickup six blocks away or was involved in the shooting at the tavern up the street. From these select bits of information, they generalize. Given the prevalence of urban street crime, there is no dearth of things for which to blame young blacks. Their own demeanor on the streets, partly a consequence perhaps of the new black self-concept coming out of the 1960s, makes young blacks likely candidates for blame. With his sneakers, "gangster cap," shades, chain necklace, and portable radio at his side, the youth is a ready candidate for distrust by those of the more conventional society. At the same time, the youth is often suspicious, if not distrustful, of those who symbolize the "square" conventions of the wider society. In general, there exists a wide social and cultural gap between young, often unskilled black youth and those who would employ them (including middle-class blacks). One might speculate that the problem of employability for young blacks of the urban environment is largely a problem of mutual distrust. Because some of the would-be employers are black, it would be incorrect to say that the distrust is based solely on racial differences. The cultural and class-related component has assumed increasing importance (Wilson, 1978). Still, race is undeniably the easiest "handle" to get on a person. It is immediately apparent and therefore figures greatly in the current stereotypes and misconceptions which affect hiring. Thus, in addition to the absence of full employment, the increased competition for available jobs, it appears to be distrust based on changing black self-concept and media stereotypes that contributes so profoundly to the intractable social problem of black youth unemployment.

Changing Black Consciousness and Civil Rights

Rosa Park's decision not to move from her seat in the front of that Montgomery bus started a new day for black Americans. As the Reverend Martin Luther King took over and formed a bus boycott that brought the city and the bus company to its knees, blacks around the country took careful note and made this event a part of their consciousness. This victory launched the Civil Rights movement. Sit-ins and other forms of social protest took place throughout the South. Blacks in the North joined in the ranks, as Reverend King marched through hostile white neighborhoods of Chicago. President John Kennedy promised great things for the blacks, which, of course, Lyndon Johnson was left to develop and carry out. The march on Washington occurred in 1963, and Civil Rights legislation was passed in 1964 and in 1968.

In Oakland, the Black Panthers began following the police around, with unloaded guns; they called their action patrolling the police, whom they considered an occupying force in the black community. The symbolic impact of all of this was tremendous. These armed black men following and watching the police presented themselves as symbols of Black Identity, and young blacks schooled in "passive resistance" took special note. The urban black ghettos around the country began to boil. Many of the most alienated ghetto blacks began to riot. Watts exploded, with heavy damage to the black community there. Significantly, their assaults were primarily against property, and not other communities; these were not "race riots" in the traditional sense; they were "property riots" (Janowitz).

This form of social protest (Hayden) or "rioting for fun and profit" (Banfield) caught on in other cities around the country. Detroit, Chicago, Cleveland, Philadelphia, New York, Baltimore, Washington, D.C., and others all had problems with the black under-class. While many were willing to define these riots as "riff-raff" opportunism, others viewed them as full-blown urban rebellions. People such as Stokely Carmichael and H. Rap Brown were accused of crossing state lines to incite these riots.

Meanwhile, blacks around the country, many of whom did not

engage in the rioting, were undergoing a social learning process. In particular, the young urban black people appeared to be moving away from a moderate, even docile, presentation of self, and began assuming a more aggressive and militant posture. Many moved from an "integrationist" and accommodative orientation toward Black Cultural Nationalism, extolling the virtues of "Blackness" and identifying more closely with their African heritage. This view spread throughout the cities and into isolated rural areas. Black leaders, locally as well as nationally, were required to inspect their views and postures on race and politics (Anderson, 1971).

While many disparate theories and ideologies existed and competed within the black community, one commonly held proposition exhorted blacks not only to look inwardly and take stock of themselves, but also to value themselves and their "Blackness" in the face of "white oppression." Parts of this movement were steeped in the rhetoric of Black Cultural Nationalism. The most extreme elements encouraged blacks toward separatism and racial particularism. From this emerged a new sense of racial pride. Many black leaders joined their followers in this pursuit. Among these leaders were Malcolm X and Elijah Muhammed. And Jesse Jackson exhorted his followers on numerous occasions to say aloud, "I am a Man" or "I may be poor, but I am Somebody." A best-selling popular record by James Brown was entitled "I'm Black and I'm Proud." All of these themes came together and generated among young blacks a new sense of self-worth. Young blacks often accepted this theme as a kind of license "to be yourself" and to loosen the bonds of dominant social institutions, eschewing their symbolic forms such as conventional dress and hairstyles. It was in these circumstances that formal and informal agencies of socialization and social control came into question. Many of the young began to dispute the authority of the police, educators, their elders, and others.

To be sure, there were many blacks, usually of middle income status or at least steadily employed, who represented the "old school" or "old guard," and who felt a commitment to the status quo, if not the status quo ante, particularly in the light of often caustic assaults against it. They were usually the ones who prided themselves on their own decency and respectability. They often felt relatively successful, that they had "done all right" by the "old way," and had fared well. They were proud and felt fine, some would say, "in their place." Their "place" had been achieved through a large amount of hard work, accommodation, and even docility, as viewed from the perspective of the now critical young; to them, this was the way they had survived in the face of racial prejudice and discrimination. The young "militant" blacks often castigated the old for being "Toms," for being repressed and even obsequious in the presence of whites. They saw these older blacks as being too constrained to speak up for their rights.

Socialized under the traditional arrangement of black and white relations, the "old-school" simply put up with such treatment that younger blacks of that day—and of today—often said they would not endure. But later, as the movement persisted, even they began to come around, infusing the movement with a certain legitimacy. Once they "understood," the older and more established members of the black community began to accept "being Black" rather than Negro. They quieted their call for the old "go slow" approach to social change and all but stopped criticizing the younger people, thinking, "Maybe they've got something to say."

Yet the young continued to chastise their elders, often blaming them and their "docility" for the inequities currently at work in society. They showed new boldness in attacking what they increasingly viewed as white-sponsored docility and exhorted the old to "stand up and be a man." Among themselves they would say (concerning the "white problem"), "I wouldn't take that stuff. I'm as good as any man." While the older blacks were thought to believe this, it seemed to take the younger people to give it the fullest expression. The "Afro" became the fashionable black hair style, taking on even political significance, and special handshakes were developed and elaborated and used among young blacks to show group solidarity and commitment to the movement (Baugh). There was the clenched fist salute which became a symbolic greeting among blacks even of only passing acquaintance. At the same time, a red, black, and green Black Nationalist flag became a symbol of black communion, if not black nationhood.

This change in the attitudes of blacks in the large urban centers of the country encouraged, even required, blacks to reinspect their values. It also demanded that they examine their relationships with whites, especially whites on the job with whom they had most personal contact. As blacks began looking at themselves, many worked at revaluation and revision of their self-concepts, trying to make them more positive and more in keeping with the demands of the movement. Many issues and questions presented themselves, the resolutions of which involved not only an inspection of self, but also attention to black group position in relationship to other groups of the social order. For young militant blacks, the most blameworthy were not always a specific ethnic group or even a particular class, but whites in general, and the blacks who "allowed themselves to be oppressed."

No other group could claim the blacks' history of slavery, poverty, and institutionalized segregation based on the laws of the land (Higginbotham). As blacks made assertions of right and clarified what they thought to be their group interests in the society, other ethnic and class groupings were required to inspect their own positions, their own relationship to the Civil Rights movement in general, and to the American black community in particular. When the "lower orders" of the stratification system begin effectively to challenge the justice of that system, moral and social questions arise for those who sense themselves to be among the higher echelons, and a feeling of unease, competitiveness, and distrust can evolve in the social and moral order. It is this set of issues that appears to have such important implications for gaining a handle on the intractable problem of black youth unemployment today.

During the 1960s, the white allies of the movement often found themselves in difficult positions. So many then claimed to be sponsors of black opportunity, they were gradually faced with a young black constituency which publicly rejected anything associated with white America, particularly white authority. At least, this was the rhetoric. Because of black attitudes, as well as many deeply ingrained white prejudices, racial integration was put on a back burner. An ethos of "black separatism" became attractive to many young blacks. At least temporarily, social mobility and middle-class orientations were viewed as "white," and thus not to be harbored, let alone emulated. For instance, in their attempts to "be Black," many young blacks proudly and often affectedly spoke "black" English and stigmatized those who spoke "standard" English, labeling it as the language of oppression. At times, "education" itself came under attack as "white." The most militant proudly embraced "Blackness," everything black was praised, and everything symbolic of white society was eschewed, if not condemned outright. Intolerance and hostility surfaced in encounters with whites, and white liberals became increasingly disenchanted with and disconnected from the movement.

Employment Problems of Young Black Males

The young black person, especially the male, both through portrayals in the mass media and, to an important degree, through personal experiences of urban whites, has come to symbolize danger and to evoke fear in the minds of many urban and suburban whites. The stereotype is now strong and is often applied indiscriminately to unknown blacks of the urban milieu. Young black men often are thought to mean trouble and are avoided, especially on the streets after dark. The "good" black, espousing middle-class values and displaying convincing middle-class emblems, is often considered to be the exception rather than the rule. He is more easily granted trust, but he too must go a very long way in order to prove himself above suspicion, particularly among white strangers (Hughes). As one well-dressed, young black delivery man told me:

> My company tries to assign blacks to black neighborhoods and whites to theirs, you know, so there won't be any misunderstandings. But I've had a lot of people stop and question me. These are black people, now. So you know it just wouldn't do for me to be making deliveries to whites. In white neighborhoods!? I wear this tie so people will put some faith in me, but even then they be checkin' me out.

The condition of trust, a condition essential to employment and to "working one's way up through the ranks" on the job, appears to be sorely lacking for the prospective young black worker. From the employer's point of view, the young black's perceived subcultural difference may be an important part of the reason he does not deserve trust on the job. Often his language is not understood or appreciated. His presentation of self, particularly his dress, often is not suitable to the employer, and, if something is said about it, the young black will probably feel he is being treated unfairly. For example, many young inner city blacks consider it perfectly normal to carry a portable radio to work, to wear sneakers, and to allow a toothpick to hang from the mouth. But such subcultural displays may be offensive to a prospective employer and make the youth eligible for his distrust. The employer is likely to view such behavior as being in need of correction and not of appreciation; it may "prove" the young worker's ignorance of what it means to work in a disciplined environment.

From the beginning, the youth is inclined to view his employer, supervisor, and fellow employees with a certain amount of suspicion. Their actions, which may be unassuming in intent, may easily be interpreted as attempts at "getting the black in line." In dealing with such a situation, some black youth will adopt a defensive posture. This was indicated in an interview with a twenty-three year old employed black man who was experiencing problems at his job as a stockman.

> These cats [bosses] try to get you in line real quick. If he think you half-stepping at all, he'll sound on you right in front of everybody. He don't care. He don't care who listening, he'll loud talk you. Don't give you no respect, no less'n you demand it. Now, see, he don't treat the whites like that. He just pick on the blacks that way. But, see, I set him straight. See, I was cool about it. I waited 'til everybody had left and I told him what was on my mind. I told him, "Now, Mr. Murphy, look. I don't appreciate the way you dressed me down in front of all the other studs. My own daddy don't do that to me in public, and I ain't 'bout to 'low you to do it. If you got something to say 'bout my work, you can tell me in private. You ain't got to broadcast it to the world, so they can cop a attitude about me." I looked him dead in his eye; he knew I was serious. I ain't had no more trouble from him. But you got to set 'em straight, 'cause if you don't, all of 'em will try to mess with you, you know.

In white-white situations where a new worker is criticized or asked to conform to some dress code or demeanor, there may be little room for the new worker to balk on racial grounds; presumably, the work rules are universal. But given the background of the 1960s and the history of racial prejudice in America, the same request made by a white boss to a young black person often leads to charges of prejudice and racial slight.

But strikingly, black supervisors employed in white-owned business can be just as exacting in their relations with black youths as white supervisors, if not more. As one nineteen year old black man employed as a pot washer and baker's helper told me:

> Ain't nothin' worse than having a black cat over you for a boss. I got this cat over me who's always on me. He worse than the white man,

always on my case. He always askin' me questions, checkin' on me, you know. He done already fired four studs off my job. What it is is that he fraid 'o the white man gettin' on him, so he stay on my case. I'm hip to him, but he just a hard person to work for. I don't know how long I'm goin' last with him.

And further, a black forty year old supermarket manager said in an interview:

Man, these black kids just don't want to work, don't know how to work. I tell you, they come to work in smelly old sneakers, cut off jeans and sweatshirts, and always got a toothpick hanging out the side of his mouth. They slouch around, I don't know, man. Sometimes I got to stop 'em from arguing among themselves. They don't seem to understand that this is a business, can't be bringin' their personal lives in here, laughing and playing around. They've got no idea of what it's all about. They look all sullen if you say the least little thing to one of 'em. They just think it's a game. They just don't know what's happenin'. They just got the wrong attitude.

Whether or not employers or supervisors act justly with regard to all employees, they are nonetheless open to the charge "racist" (in the case of whites) or of harboring "antiblack" attitudes (in the case of blacks) by black employees. The problem seems to be one of management. It may be that black untrained youth must be taught about the work setting, and that an extra measure of patience and guidance on the part of supervisors is badly needed. When a young black is criticized harshly or "unfairly," the old "self-fulfilling prophecy" (Merton) may be set in motion. The youth begins to live up (or down) to the expectations of the supervisor and other employees. When the unskilled youth is hired, he is usually expected to perform in a menial job, one of very limited responsibility and probably of high turnover. Such jobs are usually those of dishwasher, busboy, waiter, janitor, parking lot attendant, porter, etc. Moreover, because he may be lumped together with past short-term black employees who "didn't work out," and is treated as such, the youth "knows" in advance how things will turn out. There is little hope for the future.

Not only are young blacks with limited skills but high aspirations likely to view the job itself as demeaning, as racially oppressive and exploitative, but on top of it all they must often endure the watchful eyes not only of their new boss, but also of their fellow employees, people they are inclined to see as "waiting for me to mess up." In this connection, race can be significant as a device of social control within job hierarchies.

One young black cook told of a time when he was sent by the owner (with whom he was personal friends) to keep an eye on several new black employees who were thought to be stealing fifty-pound bags of flour from the basement storeroom. The head chef at the restaurant was an Asian (an illegal alien). The implication was that the Asian chef would keep his eyes on the Asian employees and the black cook would keep "his blacks" in line. The tacit threat made to the black cook by the owner of the restaurant was that if the blacks could not be kept from stealing they would have to be replaced by more trustworthy Asians. The cook, whom I interviewed, "understood" how he was being used racially by the white owner, and he also understood that blacks were for some reason more suspect in the thefts than were the "almost white" (his words) Asians. Eventually, a black dishwasher and a black pot washer were fired, and two Asians (illegal aliens) took their places.

Almost all new workers, be they menial or other laborers, must undergo a certain probationary period. The length of this period is sometimes formally set and discussed. At other times, the length is not openly discussed but is informally negotiated. In the case of those black youth who are fortunate enough even to be employed in "entry level" positions, this probationary period may never end. Many employed black youth feel permanently distrusted and suspect that fellow employees and supervisors are all too ready to collude against them and find something to hold against them. The black youth is prepared to see himself as forever the weak man and, as such, to be used as the convenient scapegoat for almost anything that goes wrong on the job. The black youth's feeling of blameworthiness generates in him a certain amount of distrust of his supervisor and fellow employees. This is illustrated in the following interview with a twenty-one year old waiter:

> My boss'll watch me like a hawk, thinking I'm gon' steal something. And it's the whites that be stealing him blind. Like, anytime somebody black comes in and I wait on 'em, the Man gon' check me out. Now, this been goin' on for two years, the cat still don't trust me. He don't do the whites that way; they come in, stay for two or three weeks and they got the run of the place. They can walk away with the whole place, but he'll blame it on me. Now, he got them watchin' me. You can tell when somebody don't trust you. I know, I can feel it, and it gets to me.

In the work setting, which requires effective cooperation, black youth often feel that their fellow employees are "always doing things" to make them look bad. They are often criticized for their work, without helpful instruction; if they ask for help, their requests are often taken as admissions of ignorance and are then held against them. They tend to fear that others are ready to report them at the slightest infraction of the rules and work standards, often imposed and enforced arbitrarily, informally, and selectively.

Further, it is not uncommon for many black workers to be treated as outsiders while on their jobs, even though they have been working on the job for a long time. Among black workers who face such problems on a common job, a standing phrase is the "can I help you?" routine. The blacks say, "When a black arrives at work, some white employee is ready with 'can I help you?'" The blacks interpret this question as a "nice" way of saying "what business do you have here?" Young black workers are sensitive to the tone of voice and the social context for the "real" meaning of the phrase. It appears to be a device of someone who is very concerned about outsiders committing a crime on the work premises. To be black and young is to be suspect. Black youth understand the nuance here, and they joke about such slights during lunch or breaks. They often gather together on the job for purposes of social defense, telling "horror" stories and communing in what they see as a hostile social and work environment.

In striving to "be Black" in the face of white authority, the black youth may consciously flout that authority. They may outwardly display a poor work attitude, ignorance, and nonacceptance of the rules of the workplace, including punctuality, subordination, and on-the-job discipline. There are many unemployed black youth who are unmotivated and uninterested in "working for a living," particularly in the dead-end jobs they are able to get. As one employed twenty-nine year old janitor told me:

> Young blacks these days just don't wanta work. Like take my younger brother. He nineteen and just graduated from high school. Now, I got him on the janitorial staff at Linden School over here on Walnut Street. You know, he worked there for three days and came back to me and said, "I can't do this work." I said, "What you mean you can't do it!?" He said, "But I got me a high school education and you mean I got to slang a mop?!" I said, "I got a high school education and I slang a mop." He didn't know what to say; he just looked at me. You know,

like all the rest o' these young boys. They don't want to work, just want something give to 'em. Aw, they'll take these little nickel and dime jobs for a while just to get some money in they pocket, but then they'll quit and go stand on the corner and try to be slick. Think they too good to work.

When they take jobs they disvalue and view as meaningless, black youth often do so grudgingly and have little patience for taking much direction and "riding" from a supervisor or from other employees who see themselves as the youth's superiors.

These status problems are very real indeed, but especially to the black youth who is often attempting to reconcile his high concept of self with the menial work he usually must perform. Such attempts at reconciliation sometimes lead to conflict between workers, making it that much easier for the other workers and the supervisor to judge young black workers as not having the "right attitude." Such conflicts are symptomatic of the person's inability or unwillingness to adjust to the demands of the workplace. Given this lack of adjustment, black youths may soon be fired or may simply stop coming around to what they consider to be a workplace hostile to blacks generally and to black youth in particular. Before leaving after the last shift, the youth may "cuss out" the employer and the others who have "made it rough" for him. Employers, in turn, may simply allow their prejudices to take over, and when considering a future black will not take "the chance." It must be noted that the black youth must adjust not only to what he probably considers menial labor, but often he must endure what he considers impossible, socially imposed work requirements designed by the staff to "keep the nigger in his place." As a result, the black youth may leave the job with bad feelings; he is either driven away by what he perceives as insults and bad treatment at the hands of his supervisor and fellow employees or he is fired outright. In either case, the result is unemployment, or withdrawal from the labor force, which constitutes a further contribution to the already large pool of jobless black youth.

Serial Employment

Even for those youths fortunate enough to be hired, such termination of employment often starts a series of bad experiences with "working for a living." They find themselves involved in "serial employment." "Working" comes to mean having one "entry level" job after another, one bad experience after another. Job mobility, then, becomes horizontal rather than vertical. In taking stock of the person's work record, the employer might see that the youth has worked two months washing dishes here, one month mopping floors there, three months busing tables at another place. The sum total of this work experience is working for a while and being let go or quitting. The youth seldom builds up a positive work experience that would provide him references which he might convincingly display to a prospective employer. In this regard, the more he works, the further behind he gets. Also, since each successive employer seems to know his "story" in advance, he is often left to the most exploitative employers. At work, he faces then the same set of problems he has faced in the past; he's been there before and "knows" what to expect from both coworkers and employer. He becomes conditioned to receiving pay that is often below the minimum wage, but he complains about this to his friends off the job or to those on the job who seem trustworthy, rather than to the proper authorities. The marginally employed youth is in no position to complain about wages and benefits when doing so would only give the employer another excuse to let him go.

For some inner city black youth, the difference between the amount earned and the minimum wage is made up by what their employers allow them to steal or accuse them of stealing. A kind of wage-theft system operates, in effect, with the tacit approval of the employer. The employer is said to set the youth's wages low with the expectation that the youth will steal a certain amount in materials from the workplace. In order to make a decent "wage," the youth in turn steals from his employer. The "self-fulfilling prophecy" is set in motion as the employer's expectations of the youth are met. Open to informal negotiation, unspoken and implicit, the arrangement lends itself to disagreements and fights between employer and employee. In such circumstances, the employer has the option of firing the youth, and often does so, at times with no pay. And in attempts to get even, the youth may return with friends to "rip-off" the employer or to vandalize the work premises. It may be that some ghetto "robberies" and "burglaries" can be attributed to just such disputes over wages.

As young black workers move from entry-level job to entry-level job, they tend to work largely for spending money, but also for money with which to make sometimes major contributions to the support of their family households. Many live within extended kinship networks whose members seek and expect financial and other forms of support from all able members (Stack). Many of the grown people in such arrangements are themselves only marginally employed and simply lack money to give to the youth. The resilience among the youth is striking in the light of numerous reports of bad prospects and problematic experiences at work. Many continue to try to find that "one good job"; yet they seldom find just what they desire. Instead, those able to find acceptable work are found in the kitchens of "good" restaurants, in pizza parlors, in "fast food" restaurants, in ghetto grocery stores, in local hardware and furniture stores, and on line at "day labor" concerns.

Getting "Good" Jobs: A Generation Gap?

While many young inner city black youth will gladly accept almost any work available, many others are said to have given up on "working," or they have become very "choicy" about the jobs they will take. Many of the older generation of blacks, for whom "hard work" and limited opportunities have been a way of life, continue to believe in the infinite availability of work and that young blacks should take what they get. They find the youth who "won't work" difficult to understand. One "hard-working" middle-aged black factory worker living alone with one of his sons told of his inability to understand his son's attitude toward working:

> I'm going through that. I got one like that. He sits around; that's why I'm moving. So, when I move this time, he better know what he's doing, 'cause I'm tellin' him, "You better get yo'self a place, 'cause I'm movin' out, now. I don't know what you got in yo' mind, but you ain't gon' laugh on me. Now, if you ain't got no place, you better find one. Now, it's up to you, now. You nineteen and if you can't find something to do, then I'm sorry. 'Cause the jobs are out there, if you want one. It may not be the kind of job you want, but it's out there. There's plenty work around. You think you so important, but you ain't no better 'n anybody else." I don't know what's the matter with that boy. But I know this. He goin' have to do somethin' 'cause I'm leaving.

While many middle-class youth might feel themselves fortunate for being able to obtain "menial" jobs, the reverse seems to be true for many inner city youth. The difference in general attitude reflects an important difference in outlook and in sense of group position within the social order. For many unskilled and skilled black youth of the urban milieu, the "menial" job takes on a profoundly different meaning. For middle-class youth, black or white, such jobs are more easily viewed as temporary and, thus, may be taken in stride. But for the inner city black youth with high aspirations and real doubts about his prospects in the labor market, such jobs are very easily viewed as "dead-end," as offering the specter of a permanent position at the bottom of the social order. Herein lies one of the fundamental reasons such jobs, even when available, are so very unappealing to numerous inner city black youth. In a real sense, black and white middle-class youth can psychologically afford to engage in "temporary" menial labor, for they are able to be relatively confident that better days are ahead. But the aspiring and often unskilled ghetto youth with a sense of sharply limited job opportunities lack faith in the prospect of "better days ahead"—the "menial" job symbolizes and promises a bleak future which is all too real in the here and now.

With meaningful employment often out of reach, the black youth in the urban area finds the streets to be an alternative source of self-esteem. At some critical point, for a young black worker even to take a menial "entry-level" job is tantamount to giving in to "failure." For taking a job often means "working" and "putting up with a lot of shit." What is of concern here is not only the issue of performing menial labor, the 1960s revaluation of self notwithstanding. Many young blacks want employment badly. The problem seems to emerge as the young black person sees himself and feels himself having to work in what he considers to be a job "beneath" him and then to have to deal psychologically with people whom he tends to see as hostile, prejudiced, and insensitive to his often loudly made claims to being a full person, an issue which he feels especially sensitive about at the present time (Goffman). As one employed black youth told me in an interview: "Brother, I go to that job, and, man, I got to catch hell from them crackers [whites] everyday I go. I get so I hate to face 'em. It's not the work, I don't mind that. It's them looks of suspicion that get to me, the treatment, you know." It is this sort of distrust of the social context of so much "entry level" employment, as well as the "bad treatment"

they receive, that many black youth find so troublesome. Many
black youth are prepared to view such jobs as occupied and con-
trolled largely by those who display the least amount of appreciation of black youth as people. Whether their assessment is
"objectively" true is not the real issue here; it matters profoundly
that so many blacks are prepared to believe this and to act on the
basis of such beliefs.

For many, the ideal concept of a "good" job is to work in an air-
conditioned office and sit behind a desk, to dress in nice clothes
and take leisurely breaks and lunch hours, and to receive "big
money" for their trouble. Though this type of job may be their
ideal, they view such jobs as reserved for whites and, in rare cases,
for blacks who have special qualifications or are just lucky. Such
jobs are very far from the reality they know and face on the streets
between consecutive menial jobs, if they are fortunate enough even
to be employed. While they desire "good" jobs, many sorely lack
basic skills, including the ability to read and write and to perform
even rudimentary computations. While possessing the high school
diploma of the segregated urban school system, many have never
acquired a basic level of education. Nonetheless, many feel they are
qualified for jobs better than those they are able to obtain.

Unskilled, untrusted, and often unwilling to adapt to the work
conditions of jobs they consider demeaning, thousands of unemployed black youth approach the labor market. As products of the
competitive urban environment, the "streets," and sometimes of
the street gangs, they often have on their minds "being tough" and
aggressively "getting over" the barriers they view the wider society
placing between them and "the good life." Fundamentally, theirs
tends to be a survival mentality shaped by persistent conditions of
poverty and racial prejudice and of never having "enough" of the
material goods they see dangled before them on television and in
the stores they visit. When they find themselves unable to "get the
jobs white people get," they tend to become all the more bitter
and alienated from the wider society. Often they have all but completely given up on the wider society and its institutions, which
they see as dominated by whites and a very few blacks who have
only recently joined them, people who they are inclined to feel
care little for them and their welfare (Wilson).

Many have all but lost hope and faith in the legitimacy of the wider society, but particularly in the whites, whom they see running it. The labor market has failed them. The schools have failed them. Only too late they come to realize the importance of schooling for getting a job; but now, they think, it is too late to do anything about their situation. As they hang on to a strand of hope, it is now that they begin to inspect the shortcomings of their own home situations, considering how things might have been different, and how that difference might have made a difference in their chances of getting a job. There is a tendency to blame oneself and one's background, but this is usually overcome by blaming "the white man" for the oppression of all blacks. While there is a certain ambivalence on this issue, the young blacks, at least for now, tend toward blaming the dominant "white" institutions and individuals they can see as the "real" stumbling blocks hindering their abilities to "get over." In this regard, they also speak constantly of "the white boy" or "the white girl" who has "an opportunity to get over," for "they people take care of 'em."

Hence, when the "Man" lets the young black worker go back to the streets, many youths view it as a kind of blessing. Being unemployed is often viewed as confirmation of what they "knew" and predisposes many to move in the direction many of their unemployed peers like to see them go—toward the underground economy.

The Underground Economy

The underground economy consists of a network of informal connections and established means by which people gain money illegally. These form a social and entrepreneurial network that spreads as a result of the participant's inability or unwillingness to participate in the regular economy. On the streets, such participation is simply referred to as a "hustle." Among themselves, participants often speak of their activities with at least a tinge of rebelliousness. Many attempt to place value on such activities; they often boast about their thefts and robberies. Within their own circles, the illegality of such enterprises often carries little or no stigma, at least not until the person is caught by authorities and "put away." Praise is usually heaped on those who can prove themselves successful, often by displaying cash and loot from a "beat" or "walk" (a group forage into the streets for the purpose of obtaining money illegally). An informal ranking system emerges through which participants can gain a degree of deference, if not solid respect, for what they claim to do well. Specialties include pimping, pickpocketing, drug dealing, fencing, strong-armed robbery, armed robbery, and confidence games. A certain aura of glamour surrounds those who are successful and are able to manage their impressions as effective participants in the underground economy. For many unemployed black youth this aura is attractive and, if pursued, may serve as an alternative to the esteem given to long-term jobholders within the black community. For those involved in the depressing condition of serial employment, active participation in the underground economy helps take up the slack during lean times and puts real money into their pockets.

As many youths find themselves moving back and forth between the two economies, degrees of involvement and commitment depend increasingly upon the opportunities and options they sense to be available to them at the time. The reality of serial employment and a sense of hopelessness borne through poor work experiences make it difficult for the young inner city black worker to recognize opportunities in the regular economy, even when they do exist. So, he tends to become distrustful of promises and hopes that in the past have turned out to be nothing more than mirages. He has been turned down for jobs or turned out of them so often that a lack of confidence in his employment abilities is a reasonable and appropriate response. With a belief in his inability to find legitimate employment, an obvious need for money, and a large amount of time on his hands, he becomes a prime candidate for a desperate means of seeking money. It is this desperation and the sense that he is unable to gain money through legitimate means without lowering his view of himself that set up the condition for him to become involved in "crime as a way of life" (Merton). So what might begin as minor involvement in "beats" and "walks" with "some of the boys" can turn into a full-time occupation, at least until a "real job" comes along.

From many interviews with employed and unemployed black youths of Philadelphia, it appears that a decision to commit a stickup or a burglary is often spontaneous in the beginning and largely dependent on the nature of one's company at the time; it often depends especially on whether they share similar experiences with and orientations toward the job market. Depending on the spirit and mood dominating the groups of young men as they leave nighttime dances and parties, they tend to be out for nothing more —or less—than a "good time." Open to suggestion, they can very easily find themselves involved in a "beat" or "taking a walk" before the night is over. The following interview is with an employed seventeen year old black male.

> It's not too hard to be involved in a "beat." Naw, not really. I'll tell you. 'Bout four or five weeks ago, me and my partners were at this dance, and we didn't have nothin' to do, so we just stood around on the corner bullshittin'. Then somebody just said, "Beat! Beat! Beat!" Then the other studs started chantin' it. Then somebody said, "You ready to walk?" The others had already started to "walk." So, I said, "Yeah, I'm ready to walk." I guess I just didn' wanta be left out, you know. To go on a "beat" is to go out and have some fun and get some money from somebody, you know? When somebody say, "Let's walk," then that's just what that means. You know, go out and get it, some money off somebody. Well, we met this old lady on this street and somebody said, "Let's get her." But then somebody else say, "Aw, naw. Man, that might be her rent money." Just like that, the guys figured they'd let her slide and went off lookin' for somebody else to mess with. I just split off from 'em, 'cause I just didn't wanta get in no trouble that night. I knew just what they was headed for. I split.

Although a daredevil mentality often governs the criminal act and helps it to appear as "fun," it is important to note that such street crimes are really extreme measures, engaged in more than coincidentally by young people with no other means of obtaining money. The offenders feel they have little stake in established, civilized society and have little to lose by continuing such behavior. They have been affected by the socioeconomic system in such a way that they feel little moral obligation to it and to those supporting it. They are indeed alienated and find sanction and communion primarily among those who think similarly. It is within such groupings of the underground that reputation is to be gained, social status acquired, and deference and respect to be aspired to and earned.

Moreover, these youth have developed an elaborate ideology in order to justify their criminal adaptation to the dire situation of no job and no money. This ideology portrays "getting by" without work as virtuous. It venerates the successful criminal, the big-time gangster, the pimp, the successful entertainer, and even the famous prizefighter. It selects as role models not those pointed to as heroes by the respectable society, but those who appear to "get big money" and "get over" by any means other than hard work at a regular job. Under employment conditions different than those which exist in the present society, just such a regular job might be pursued and possibly obtained. Their fathers, uncles, and older relatives followed such jobs successfully. But many of the youth have sworn off commitments to work hard at just any job available, in the spirit of an earlier generation of blacks. They want something "better." Also, many have tried the route of the older generation and "failed." Not only was the work not there, but also this generation of black youth is not inclined to take "the stuff" their forefathers took on the job in their interactions with whites. Often unable to find work, they emphasize what might be called "counter-work ethic" values, and, by so doing, unemployed youth are able to rationalize their inability to get work. From an initial "sour grapes" attitude toward work, a full-blown counter-ideology develops.

Even so, the work ethic seems deeply ingrained among employed or unemployed black youth. Many marginally involved street criminals will go looking for a regular job whenever they hear about one, thus giving the lie to the often repeated statement that black youth do not want to work. Often they will at least try it out. But in attempting to value his unemployed status, the youth will tell his friends he does not have to work, that he can "get by" without having to "slave" for the "Man." And by passing himself off on the corner as someone who does not have to work, he seeks to draw attention away from the fact that he was unsuccessful at finding suitable work. He lets others know that he is choosy about the work he will do. Crucial to an understanding of this young black male is the notion that the more he presents himself as one "who ain't got to work," the more of a stake he gains in pretending to the activities of the underground economy. Commitment to "the street" may grow incrementally (Becker). And at some point, the person's identity is likely to become so bound up with crime that were an opportunity for a "good" job to come along, he might have to turn it down in order to save face among peers.

In approaching an understanding of the intractable social problem of black youth unemployment, a number of general factors need to be taken into account. Much attention has been focused on black youth over the past two decades, by lawmakers, universities, the media, and by blacks themselves. A new conception of the black man in America has grown out of so much public and private concern. The newly emerging picture, be it widely applicable to blacks or not, is that of an assertive, struggling young person who will not "take the shit" his forefathers did. This new black person is especially sensitive to what could be construed as racial prejudice, slight, and discrimination. Self-consciously aspiring toward personal independence and self-respect, many young blacks see themselves and are seen by others as not taking "the stuff" that traditionally has been dished out to black Americans. "Stand up to the Man" is perhaps a paraphrase of the legacy of the Civil Rights movement and the ghetto riots of the 1960s. Add to this new image of militancy the growing problem of youth unemployment and a stereotype of black youth as being primarily responsible for urban street crime, street gang activity, and general incivility, and one is faced with the specter of a nearly "unemployable" person. Black youths are viewed as dangerous by most people who must make use of the urban environment, including many blacks themselves. Even the "regulars on the corner," the members of the groups who partake, if only minimally, of the rewards of the regular economy, will say "these young jitterbugs [youth] bear watchin'" (Anderson, 1978).

Most importantly, black youth need to be provided with job skills and training in order to become self-supporting and socially independent. At present, many view themselves as having no real stake in the society and nothing to lose by engaging in antisocial behavior and crime. At the same time many are moving into a phase of life that can only lead, if not tended to with job skills and jobs, to a real inability to function in a work setting. At present, many employers do not want to take a chance on black youth, the black adult population of tomorrow, but such chances must be taken. At the same time, the employers will have to display tolerance, patience, and understanding toward the black youth, who are already deeply suspicious of the job marketplace in which he is already beginning to accumulate a series of bad experiences with "work."

Large scale formal organizations must be sensitive to the mobility and status needs of young inner city blacks. They must work to insure that people are treated with respect on the job, even those in the most menial of jobs. This is necessary to support their making the transition from joblessness to a state of employment. To the youth, it must be pointed out that their years of work will lead somewhere and that their jobs are meaningful. Often the problems of blacks within large organizations tend to be those of personnel. Many such problems possibly could be alleviated if supervisors could be more sensitive to the status problems of black youth working under them. Moreover, advancement on the job must be possible. In all of these areas, business organizations should be able to take a larger role in working to break down the barriers of race prejudice and discrimination within the ranks of lower level employees, for this is where many of the problems experienced among black youth are sensed to be.

Because of their inability to get "good" jobs, many black youth feel a deep sense of failure and of being "outside" American society. If the employment situation continues with respect to black youth, this sense of failure and "outsideness" will probably lead to increasing bitterness, hostility, and more alienation from American society. Crime and violence in the urban areas will rise as an increasingly angry and unruly black male population matures. The unemployed black youth are in desperate straits, and this can only lead to the undermining of civilized urban society. Already, parks and other public areas are off-limits to urban residents after dark, and urban streets are by no means safe. The condition can only worsen as the black youth take their places as part of the "permanent" American under class. To build the necessary commitment to society, the youth need meaningful employment. They do not need "make work" jobs, but jobs that teach them useful money-making skills; without these skills provided by the wider society, the youth will develop a tendency to learn the skills of the underground in order to survive. At this time, there are many youth who would jump at the chance to work, even those who appear committed to the underground economy; they would much rather work in legitimate occupations. If given the chance, many of these youth will grow into productive, law-abiding citizens. Without that chance, they might grow into criminals and help fill the prisons of the land. What they need most is a stake in the society, and a skill or a trade or an occupation is the best way in which that stake may be granted.

The American occupational structure has persisted for too long in keeping black youth at a distance, contributing not only to the "outsider" status of blacks in their own society, but also to the consolidation of what promises to be a permanent under class of socially and spiritually alienated black Americans.

Bibliography

ANDERSON, ELIJAH, *A Place on the Corner*. Chicago: University of Chicago Press, 1978.

———, "Black Shadow Politics in Midwestville," *Sociological Inquiry* (winter 1971).

BANFIELD, EDWARD, *The Unheavenly City*. Boston: Little, Brown, 1970.

BAUGH, JOHN, "The Politics of the Black Power Handshakes," *Natural History* (October 1978).

BECKER, HOWARD S., "Notes on the Concept of Commitment," *American Journal of Sociology* (July 1960).

DAVIS, ALLISON, "The Motivation of the Underprivileged Worker," in *Industry and Society*, ed., William F. Whyte. New York: McGraw-Hill, 1946.

GOFFMAN, ERVING, *Stigma*. Englewood Cliffs, N.J.: Prentice-Hall, 1963.

HAYDEN, TOM, *Rebellion in Newark*. New York: Random House, 1967.

HIGGINBOTHAM, LEON, *In the Matter of Color*. New York: Oxford University Press, 1978.

HUGHES, EVERETT C., "Dilemmas and Contradictions of Status," *American Journal of Sociology* (March 1945).

JANOWITZ, MORRIS, "Patterns of Collective Racial Violence," in *Political Conflict*, ed., Janowitz. New York: Quadrangle Books, 1970.

MERTON, ROBERT K., *Social Theory and Social Structure*. New York: Free Press, 1957.

STACK, CAROL, *All Our Kin*. New York: Harper & Row, 1974.

WILSON, WILLIAM J., *The Declining Significance of Race*. Chicago: University of Chicago Press, 1978.

Ernst W. Stromsdorfer

4

The Effectiveness of Youth Programs:

An Analysis of the Historical Antecedents of Current Youth Initiatives

Introduction: The Policy Issue

The problem of youth unemployment and the related problem of improving the schooling and training experience of youth are longstanding, and few solutions have been identified. The unemployment problem has developed over several decades. At least a portion of this problem threatens to continue even into the next decade when the proportion of youth in the population will decline.

DR. ERNST W. STROMSDORFER *is vice president of Abt Associates, Inc., a social science research firm. After teaching at Penn State and then Indiana University, he joined the Office of the Assistant Secretary for Policy Education and Research—Department of Labor as deputy assistant secretary for Research and Evaluation. Dr. Stromsdorfer has written numerous articles in the area of labor economics and youth employment.*

The youth unemployment problem is most severe among black youths. Black youths have a higher incidence of unemployment than white youths. Their unemployment duration is longer; their labor force participation is lower; and their employment/population ratio is lower (see Figure 1).

The labor force and employment condition of teenage black females has been the worst in absolute and relative terms for the past twenty-five years. However, the condition of black males has shown the most severe deterioration. Twenty-five years ago their employment/population ratio was slightly higher than that of teenage white males. Currently, it is about one-half that of teenage white males. Over a decade ago the employment/population ratio of teenage black males fell below that of teenage white females.

A combination of demand and supply factors has been identified as the principal cause of this youth joblessness. But the proportionate contribution of each factor, such as racial discrimination by employers or poor work attitudes of youth, to suggest two issues, has not been rigorously determined. It is important to rank these causes, however, since each suggests different policy recommendations. We judge, though, that the strong ethnic differences which exist indicate a significant structural rather than a cyclical unemployment problem. (See the discussions by Freeman and Wachter in this volume.)

Based on the judgment that the basic problem is structural, the general focus of social policy to counteract youth unemployment, and its short-term and long-term effects, is to increase a person's employment, training and education, or both, by a variety of training subsidies, employment subsidies, and supportive services, such as counseling, job placement, or health care, to suggest a few. The program solutions should be targeted and highly focused.

The purpose of this chapter is to examine the programs established in the Youth Act of 1977 to determine if they are likely to contribute to a solution of these structural problems. By looking at the labor market and educational results of the historical antecedents of the Youth Act, we may judge the likelihood that these revisions and extensions of earlier youth employment and training programs will alleviate the labor market problems faced by youths at this time.

Youth Initiatives

THE RATIONALES FOR CURRENT PROGRAMS

Past and current programs to better the schooling and labor market experience of youth have multiple objectives, some of which complement each other and some of which are mutually conflicting. There are several reasons for this:

1. The problems themselves are very complex. There are multiple causes of the problems. The causes may interact in undefined ways. Their nature and solution are not well understood.
2. Because of the multiple causes of these problems, an attempted solution to one aspect of the problem, say, provision of a large number of low-wage jobs to cool down the "long hot summer" may result in provision of jobs that have little or no on-the-job training content or may result in the provision of "dead-end" jobs that serve as little more than an excuse for income transfer. However, the provision of better quality jobs may have the perverse effect of increasing the rate at which youths drop out of school.
3. The problems extend beyond the socioeconomic classes immediately affected. For instance, youth unemployment and crime are highly correlated. Both lead to the economic instability and personal insecurity of third parties.
4. The problems may have effects over a person's life cycle beyond the immediate stage when they first appear to be chronic.

Thus, it is understandable that the approaches by Congress and the executive branch to the solution of the youth schooling and employment problem are multifocused and diffused.

The complex and diffuse nature of these proposed policies severely complicates the process of evaluating the programs' effectiveness. For instance, the effect of a program may be to:

1. increase a youth's employability,
2. change the distribution of income,
3. reduce crime, and
4. reduce the premarital birth rate.

There is no metric whereby the social importance of each of these effects can be compared. Some of the benefits and costs of the program may have social or psychological dimensions which cannot yet

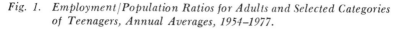

Fig. 1.   *Employment/Population Ratios for Adults and Selected Categories of Teenagers, Annual Averages, 1954–1977.*

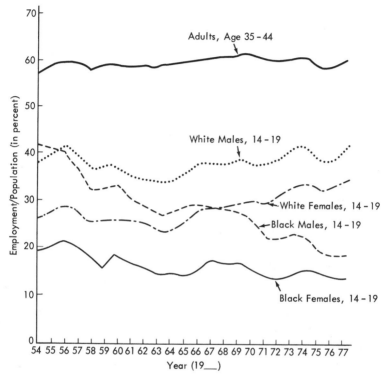

Source: Orley Ashenfelter, "What Do Teenage Unemployment Statistics Measure?"

be meaningfully measured. For instance, one can evaluate the change in property loss due to a change in the juvenile crime rate, but how does one evaluate the change in the mental state of the past or potential crime victims or the change in social values of the youth who may perpetuate crimes? (See Mallar.)

In short, the relative inability to measure certain crucial outcomes of youth programs has resulted in the dominance, for policy purposes, of economic outcomes which can be evaluated in monetary terms. This latter phenomenon has had other effects. Namely, there has been a tendency to treat such programs as vocational edu-

cation and employment and training programs as investments designed to increase earnings and employability, even though such a
focus represents only part of the objectives of such programs. In
effect, the government, while aware of the ambiguity surrounding
our understanding of how education or training might improve
labor market experience, has set up policies under the assumption
that such treatments are causally and positively related to increased
earnings and employment.

It is instructive to look at each of the existing major youth training programs to determine whether such a precise conceptual ra-
tionale is appropriate to their actual structure and, if so, how each
program is intended to achieve its objectives. It is easier to test the
effectiveness of a program which has a precise objective and operational structure than to test a program which either has a diffuse
set of competing and complementary objectives or which applies a
diffuse approach to the amelioration of schooling or labor market
disabilities. The modeling of anticipated effects is a necessary first
step in identifying programs which work and the way in which
they work. Not withstanding the constraints imposed by multiple
objectives, our basic judgment is that employment and training
programs have not always been well-designed in the past, both from
the standpoint of structuring and delivering services to clients and
also from the standpoint of discovering the effects of these treatments.

A principal cause for weakness in the structure and delivery of
program services stems from legitimate political concerns—a perceived need to do a little something for everyone and pressure for
a "quick fix" to complex social problems. The weakness of analysis
of program effects is partly a function of this diffuse approach—
a large variety of services is delivered across a broad target population but in amounts which may not constitute a critical mass to
change conditions (Mangum and Walsh). In addition, the problem
of discovering if a program works is increased by what has often
been an inadequate use of analytic design and statistical method.
With these thoughts in mind, we proceed to a discussion of the
design of the current youth programs.

This discussion focuses on the degree of specificity of the target
group, the existence of a program structure that relates program
treatments to implicit or explicit outcomes, and the nature of con-

straints imposed on the program. Table 1 outlines the major program characteristics as these are described in the existing laws.

The Young Adult Conservation Corps (YACC) is intended to give young persons experience in a variety of occupational skills by means of productive work on conservation and other projects on federal and nonfederal lands and waters.

The target population for the Young Adult Conservation Corps encompasses *all* socioeconomic groups. One need only be unemployed to gain employment under the program. Apart from providing a subsidized job plus additional services, the program provides informal on-the-job training (see Table 1). The quantitative and qualitative impact of this training is limited by the constraint of a twelve-month maximum enrollment period. It is further limited by the requirement that the jobs be labor intensive and basically provide seasonal and part-time employment experience. Hence, there is a potential internal conflict in this program which drives the program more toward its equity goal (which in itself is not well specified—every socioeconomic group can qualify) and away from its efficiency goal. (For this discussion, the term "equity" refers to the structure and changes in the structure of the income distributor. "Efficiency" refers to the level and changes in the level of worker productivity as evidenced by earnings and employability.)

The Youth Community Conservation and Improvement Projects are designed to develop the vocational preparation of jobless youth through well-supervised work of tangible community benefit. However, this program has problems similar to the YACC—a constrained period of work experience focused on labor intensive projects. Thus the quantity and quality of on-the-job training is low. However, the complementarity between schooling and work is recognized in that placement in subsidized jobs is to be coordinated with the school system and the employment service. The possibility of receiving academic credit for work experience exists in this program. Thus, the program has elements of a cooperative vocational education program—a longstanding secondary and postsecondary educational format.

The Youth Incentive Entitlement Pilot Projects program has one

Table 1. The Operational Structure of Existing Employment and Training Programs to Serve Youth

	Young Adult Conservation Corps	Youth Incentive Entitlement Pilot Projects	Youth Community Conservation and Improvement Projects
Target population	•all social and economic backgrounds •unemployed, but preference given to the structurally unemployed •age 16–23 inclusive •citizens, permanent residents or lawful refugees or parolees	•economically disadvantaged as defined by Office of Management and Budget Guidelines •dropouts or dropout prone •age 16–19 •structurally unemployed	•out-of-school •unemployed •age 16–19
Constraints	•enrollment not to exceed 12 months •dropping out of school to enter program is prohibited	•projects to last not less than 6 months or more than 9 •unlimited attendance over the high school enrollment period	•enrollment not to exceed 12 months
Main nature of activity	•labor intensive •similar to activities of persons engaged in seasonal and part-time employment •academic credit potentially may be awarded •on-the-job training	•minimum wage job if and only if a person returns to school •part-time in-school and full-time during summer	•labor intensive •work experience with school-related credits, including post-secondary education
Supplementary services	•transportation •lodging •subsistence •medical treatment	•apprenticeship •counseling •medical treatment •transportation •day care •institutional training	•coordination with school systems and employment services •job training •skill development
Designed impact on participants	•secure unsubsidized employment by giving experience in various occupational skills	•high school graduation or its equivalent, leading to improved post-program employment, education, or both	•secure unsubsidized employment through work experience, skill training, and community service

Source: "Youth Employment and Demonstration Projects Act of 1977," Public Law 95–93, 95th Congress, August 5, 1977 and "Comprehensive Employment and Training Act Amendments of 1978," Public Law 95–524, 95th Congress, October 27, 1978.

Youth Employment and Training Programs	Summer Youth Employment Program	Job Corps
•economically disadvantaged: 85% or less of the Bureau of Labor Statistics lower living standard •unemployed or structurally unemployed •age 16–21, with 14 & 15 year olds under special authority •in-school and out-of-school youths	•economically disadvantaged: 70% or less of the Bureau of Labor Statistics lower living standard •age 14 through 21	•economically disadvantaged as defined by Office of Management and Budget Guidelines •age 14 through 21 •living in an environment which impairs performance •persons on probation or parole
•none specifically stated	•no enrollment in program activities beyond September 30 of each year	•age constraints waived for the handicapped •two years enrollment plus waivers
•combined employment, community service, training and supportive services linked with school attendance and certification where possible	•on-the-job training •job exploration	•residential and non-residential education and work experience
•training, education and labor market information •literacy and bilingual training •job sampling •GED certification •transportation •child care •apprenticeship •institutional training •on-the-job training •job restructuring •placement services	•academic credit for work experience •vocational counseling and occupational information	•physical rehabilitation •travel and leave allowances •GED certification •readjustment allowances •residential subsistence •counseling and testing •required participation in Center maintenance •recreation
•reduce structural unemployment and secure suitable unsubsidized employment	•obtain unsubsidized employment and develop maximum occupation potential	•improve future employment and earnings and educational possibilities

Notes: A complete catalog of programs to aid youth is contained in Lawrence, Johnson and Associates, Inc., *Catalog of Federal Youth Programs,* Division of Youth Activities, Office of Youth Development, Office of Human Development, U.S. Dept. of Health, Education, and Welfare, Washington, D.C.

of the most interesting rationales. It is designed to aid youth in completing high school by providing subsidized jobs at the federal minimum wage as a matter of entitlement if and only if a person will return to high school or pursue its equivalent. That is, in its demonstration sites, the program has been given sufficient funds to serve *all* eligibles who apply. Here, the federal government is an employer-of-last-resort. It is well targeted on economically disadvantaged dropout prone youth. Next, while projects within the program are limited in length, enrollment in the program can continue as long as one is less than age twenty and has not yet graduated from high school. Thus, the "quick fix" bias of the previous two programs is avoided and the potential complementarity between education and work is recognized. However, while the intermediate goal of the program is quite explicit—high school graduation or its equivalent—it is less clear as to why high school graduation is so desirable or what it is likely to lead to. Obviously, one can argue that insofar as high school graduation improves productivity (or has other positive effects), it may lead to improved education or employment after graduation. This ultimate result is recognized but does not receive extensive formal attention in the law.

There are potential conflicts in the program, however, since education and work compete for one's energy and time in the short run. A person may go back to school once guaranteed a job but may cut back on the quality or quantity of his or her education by reducing the difficulty or number of courses or by spending less time in school. The success of the program will likely depend on the enforcement of scholastic standards, including academic and attendance, and job performance standards. Program design and management problems interact.

Analysis of the preenrollment labor market experience of a sample of youth eligible for this program demonstrates that short-run trade-offs exist between working and schooling (Barclay et al.). It is simplistic to consider the problem of youth dropout and unemployment behavior as a linear process of "transition from school to work." Over the age range in question, school and work can exist side by side in a variety of formats. Thus, because of the complexity of choices among schooling, market work, homework, leisure, and other activities, as well as the dynamic changes that occur over the sixteen through nineteen year age range, the different ages cannot be treated as one homogeneous group. These and other important phenomena are not specifically recognized in the law. As a result, the evaluation of this program becomes more complex even though the program itself has a surface simplicity.

In contrast to the apparent simplicity of the Youth Entitlement Program, the Youth Employment and Training Program offers a complex menu of training and supportive services, including apprenticeship, GED certification, job sampling, and transportation subsidies, to list a few items. These services are intended to enhance the job prospects and career preparation of low-income youth who have the most severe employment problems. Each of the program services can have a positive effect on employability, but it becomes almost impossible in practice to sort out the net contribution of each. In practice, clients receive a mix of these treatments. Small sample sizes for the large number of treatment combinations, research cost constraints, and the absence of random assignment of clients among program treatments make such programs difficult to evaluate. Thus, while it may be reasonable to provide a program of this nature, an unambiguous analysis of its effects is unlikely. The effects of any one program component, such as receipt of a GED certificate, will be confounded with other program treatments. In such a situation there is a significant chance of erroneously rejecting a beneficial program.

Similar in some respects to the above program is the Job Corps, for it, too, offers a large set of intensive vocational education services and other treatments designed to remove labor market, educational, health, or other personal disabilities. The program has the distinguishing characteristic of a large residential component. Major program focus is on classical vocational education in a structured environment.

Finally, the Summer Youth Employment Program, of all the programs discussed here, has the least structure. It is intended to be an on-the-job training program of limited duration, but it is also intended to help meet a youth's current income needs. Experience with its predecessor, the Summer Program for Employment of Disadvantaged Youth, suggests that, as a result of management and other problems, the on-the-job training component may have been badly diluted. However, as the program has operated in the past, its focus has been mainly to achieve equity goals and directly or indirectly reduce social tensions.

In summary, the youth programs that exist offer various combinations and intensities of subsidized work, training, and other services. Like their predecessors, they operate in a difficult environment and often must be put into operation without sufficient time to ensure adequate management. Thus, although they have enrolled many youth, the lasting effect they have had is an open question. And only the Youth Entitlement Program and the Job Corps have been designed in such a way as to permit adequate investigation.

PAST EXPERIENCE OF PROGRAM ANTECEDENTS

There is a large evaluation literature covering the historical antecedents of the above programs (Mangum and Walsh, Perry, Stromsdorfer, Taggart). Most of this research, while informative about various aspects of any given program—especially institutional and operational experience—does not give unchallengeable guidance on program effectiveness.

The problems with program evaluation begin with the program management information systems. Thus, the study by Perry et al., notes that "comprehensive data on the number and nature of persons served by the JOBS program are virtually nonexistent and the data which are available are of questionable reliability and validity." More recently, there is considerable error in the cost and enrollment data reported for the Comprehensive Employment and Training Act programs. Though at the aggregate level this error tends to cancel out, individual project error can be significant and can damage efforts to assess the program. More importantly, as the current data are reported, it is not possible to generate a three-way cross-classification of (a) the number of clients described by socio-demographic status as a function of (b) program treatment and (c) cost outlay. Thus, basic information on who receives what quantity of services is seriously deficient.

The second problem with the quality of our evaluative information results from the preference for case studies of program process, with major focus on the details of program installation and operation. These are certainly not trivial concerns, but the dominant interest of government officials in such studies displaces program-wide studies of the overall long-run social impact of employment and training programs. In fact, a proper evaluation always requires a process study to describe the program delivery system or mechanism for transforming social resources into program benefits. However, the extant process studies often do not capture the key elements of this mechanism, and a taste for these types of studies nurtures a bias against classical randomized experiments of employment and training programs.

Failure to use random design results in the inability to assert cause and effect between program treatment and outcomes. Perhaps the most convincing nonexperimental study of the impact of institutional training programs has been done by Ashenfelter. Ashenfelter used an extensive time series on preprogram, during, and postprogram social security earnings to measure program impact. But he, too, points out that his results may suffer, as do all but a few studies in this area, from selection bias.

> A second difficulty that must be coped with is the obvious problem of the selection bias in program participation that shows up clearly in these results. This problem may be extreme with respect to female trainees whose employment status may be the cause rather than the result of entrance to training. One solution to this problem would be to rely on more careful sample design with an explicit control on the selection procedure for program participation, but this approach has met enormous resistance by program managers. An alternative approach may be to study the selection procedure more explicitly in the hope of identifying its structure.

In summary, the main conceptual and technical problems are:

1. inadequate and inaccurate program fiduciary data,
2. a plethora of process and case studies from which it is difficult to generalize to the program as a whole, and
3. the absence of classical random design to guarantee the unbiasedness of program effect.

Because of these problems, we discuss only the most recent and reliable studies of each of the major programs. Surveys of the literature will be used to glean judgments from the remaining vast literature.

The Youth Incentive Entitlement Pilot Projects program is an outgrowth of the in-school and summer Neighborhood Youth Corps. Originally, the main objective of both these programs was to reduce the school dropout rate. Rather soon, this objective was dropped for the summer component. The underlying operational principle of these two programs was not clearly stated in the original legislation or regulations, but one can infer a perception that the opportunity costs (foregone wages) of attending school are significant and large—especially for poor children. The strong association among the business cycle, unemployment, and school attendance was seen as evidence of this. Thus, it was hoped the provision of a subsidized job would increase the probability that youth will stay in school or return to school. There was also concern that much of the teenage unemployment problem is due to lack of realistic exposure to the world of work, with the consequence that teenagers have poor work habits. Thus, operationally, these programs became "a work experience program of variable length with a minimal training component" (Mooney).

Analysis of the two programs did not demonstrate the desired school retention effect (Mangum and Walsh). As a partial result, we have in the Youth Entitlement program the tied sale of school and work as a major program revision—one can have a subsidized job at the federal minimum wage if and only if one returns to school or pursues its equivalent. A youth must also maintain some minimal level of scholastic and work performance. The key to this program may be enforcement of the minimal level of scholastic and work performance, for Mangum and Walsh note that work experience alone "has no appreciable effect on the employability of enrollees."

Smith and Pitcher also surveyed the literature on the Neighborhood Youth Corps. Their conclusions about its overall impact on long-run employment and earnings are also negative. In particular, they pointed out that an earlier study by Somers and Stromsdorfer which reported positive effects was seriously flawed.

Although this data set represented a national stratified random sample of in-school and summer Neighborhood Youth Corps participants and a similarly selected comparison group, it was severely compromised by nonresponse bias and selection bias. In addition, later efforts to correct the errors in the Somers and Stromsdorfer estimates were subject to considerable instability. Thus, this study failed to assess the program.

Finally, a case study by Robin of the in-school and summer Neighborhood Youth Corps for black female teenagers in Cincinnati which used random assignment into the program found no positive school attendance effects. These were reliable findings, but the analysis is, of course, specific to the context of Cincinnati at that historical time.

One configuration of the Youth Entitlement program is to structure it in the form of a cooperative vocational education program. Such a program is characterized by simultaneous (as with Youth Entitlement) or alternating work and schooling periods. Stromsdorfer and Fackler analyzed such a program in Dayton, Ohio. In this study, comparisons were made among the cooperative vocational curriculum, the standard vocational curriculum, the academic or college preparatory curriculum, and the general curriculum. The analysis was split out by a combination of sex, ethnic, and class cohort combinations. As with most of the studies we discuss, the findings of this study are distorted by selection bias insofar as persons of different tastes, skills, and innate abilities select themselves into different curricula. Also, this is a case study which is specific to the historical context in Dayton.

For different measures of earnings and employment and varying sociodemographic and educational cohorts, the cooperative vocational education curriculum does not have positive and statistically significant effects. But, in general there are no striking major differences among the curricula and the cooperative program does not have an overwhelming advantage vis-à-vis the other curricula. In addition, as has been noted in other studies of training and vocational education, the main positive effects of the cooperative-vocational curriculum decay rapidly over time. The results show that what mattered in the first few years out of secondary school was whether one took some type of coherent vocational education curriculum and not whether this training occurred in the context of a cooperative vocational program. Both variants of vocational training dominated the academic curriculum, though the dominance declined over time. These specific findings are substantiated by a survey of a wider variety of literature by Mangum and Walsh.

Effects for Black Youths—Since the youth unemployment problem is most severe for black youths, it is instructive to note the effects of the several curricula on the labor market performance of black youths. Briefly, across a series of models which estimate labor market behavior, only the vocational curriculum (but not the cooperative nature of vocational education) yields a net advantage to black males. This effect is for wage rates, which suggests a net increase in the student's productivity. This analysis, however, is marred by very small sample sizes for black youth, a factor which could account for the overall lack of estimated effects for blacks. The survey by Mangum and Walsh reports even less favorable results for disadvantaged youth in general.

The Summer Youth Employment Program is related to the summer Neighborhood Youth Corps and is a recent revision of the Summer Program for Economically Disadvantaged Youth. Early in the experience of the summer Neighborhood Youth Corps it became apparent to Congress that this program would not likely realize its educational objectives. Thus, as noted above, the summer Neighborhood Youth Corps came to be rationalized as an income redistribution program to "cool off the long hot summer." The efficiency goal of the program was subordinated to a broader set of social goals. The impact of the program became correspondingly more difficult to evaluate.

The 1979 General Accounting Office (GAO) study of the Summer Program for Economically Disadvantaged Youth, though based on a very small judgment sample of prime sponsors, and therefore not necessarily a valid assessment of the program as a whole, uncovered severe management problems, particularly in the large urban areas. The short-term, annual quick start-up nature of the program is partly responsible for these severe management problems. However, there may be a more fundamental reason for the alleged fiduciary and management problems with this program. This reason may be that the immediate focus of this program is on income maintenance —pure equity concerns—rather than on the educational and on-the-job training goals which are stressed for the program in the GAO report. If, in the popular mind, a program is mainly supposed to keep kids off the streets, redistribute income in cash form, or both, then the pressure to deliver more substantive long-run results will be diluted. It may be a mistake, therefore, to stress the equity or income maintenance aspects of a multiobjective program at the expense of the efficiency aspects of improving the productivity of youth and, thus, their labor market performance. We agree with Mangum and Walsh that even in these kinds of programs useful work should be done. And, indeed, Mangum and Walsh stress that work experience programs (as well as other youth programs) should not be overloaded with unmotivated and seriously disadvantaged youth. This, of course, poses a dilemma since such youth represent a major target group for youth programs. No solution to this dilemma is obvious at this time.

The Job Corps—The Job Corps is one of the few youth programs which has shown considerable survivability, though it got off to a rocky start and was also under direct attack by President Nixon for a time. The earliest, and for almost a decade, the best evaluation of the Job Corps was done by Glen G. Cain, largely using indirect data sources. Cain estimated a range of cost-benefit ratios for this program, the central value of which was close to unity. Thus, the program's justification on efficiency grounds was insecure. However, recent work bears out the positive, though small, benefit estimates made by Cain (Mallar et al.). Mallar's initial results deal with the short-term period (initial seven months) after program exit. The Job Corps participants as a group had average weekly earnings of $4.50 more per week as compared to their comparison groups. Job Corps participants who completed their program training had earning gains of twenty-three dollars per week more than their comparison group counterparts. In general, more had obtained employment, attended college, or joined the military. In addition, they had greater health and mobility. Finally, dependence on transfer programs was reduced, and there was a reported reduction in criminal behavior and reduced drug and alcohol abuse. Cost-benefit ratios for the program were positive but depended heavily (50 percent) on reported reductions in criminal behavior, the net monetary benefits of which were indirectly estimated with secondary data. We judge that, among the studies of programs which estimate labor market effects, the results of Mallar, as he argues, are relatively robust.

Sex and Ethnicity—Mallar's results show that white and Hispanic males had higher benefits in terms of employment and earnings than did black and American Indian males. For instance, white males had an increased probability of postprogram employment of .175 while for black males the increased probability was .119. In terms of earnings, the gains were about forty-five dollars per week for white males but only about twenty-six dollars per week for black males. There were no statistically significant sex-ethnic labor market effects for females without children, however.

In summary, based on the work of Mallar et al., and backed up by a judgment by Mangum and Walsh who reviewed a number of less sophisticated studies, the Job Corps is, apparently, a reasonable model for alleviating the labor market problems of youth.

Institutional Training—This is a major component of five of the six youth programs encompassed under the Youth Act. Two studies, one by Ashenfelter and the other by Kiefer, stand out methodologically. Accordingly, we report these here, even though the results for institutional training in these studies are not youth specific. Ashenfelter's method is to use a time series of Social Security earnings data reported on a national sample of institutional trainees and a comparison group. Preprogram earnings are used to control for postprogram differences in earnings which are not due to training. Because the preprogram earnings history is so extensive, and since it should capture most of the preprogram differences in productivity and employability between trainees and the comparison group, these findings are robust.

While Ashenfelter does not report separate results by age, he does report effects by sex-ethnic categories.

> . . . although there remains considerable ambiguity of interpretation, training does appear to have increased the earnings of all trainee groups. For males this effect is between $150 and $500 (per annum) in the period immediately following training but declining to perhaps half this figure after five years. For females this effect is between $500 and $600 in the period immediately following training and does not seem to decline in the succeeding years.

TABLE 2. ESTIMATED TRAINING EFFECTS (AND ESTIMATED STANDARD ERRORS) USING DIFFERENT BASE PERIODS FOR VARIOUS GROUPS OF MDTA TRAINEES

Train-ing Effect in	Black Males Base Period Is			White Females Base Period Is			Black Females Base Period Is		
	1961	1962	1963	1961	1962	1963	1961	1962	1963
1962	−18 (21)			−88 (15)			−22 (18)		
1963	−248 (26)	−231 (21)		−317 (20)	−238 (15)		−165 (24)	−146 (19)	
1964	−454 (32)	−439 (29)	−273 (25)	−412 (24)	−349 (22)	−142 (17)	−154 (29)	−139 (26)	−25 (22)
1965	318 (38)	331 (36)	470 (34)	354 (28)	408 (26)	572 (24)	441 (36)	456 (34)	552 (32)
1966	372 (48)	393 (46)	530 (45)	364 (34)	414 (33)	559 (31)	517 (44)	532 (43)	627 (41)
1967	198 (52)	218 (51)	337 (50)	409 (38)	452 (37)	576 (36)	460 (51)	475 (50)	563 (48)
1968	93 (62)	115 (61)	235 (60)	365 (43)	405 (42)	514 (42)	364 (58)	379 (57)	465 (56)
1969	126 (67)	146 (66)	259 (66)	496 (47)	535 (46)	636 (46)	419 (65)	433 (64)	527 (63)

Source: Orley Ashenfelter, "Estimating the Effect of Training Programs on Earnings," *The Review of Economics and Statistics,* Vol. LX, No. 1, February 1978, Table 6.

We should also note that the effect is much less favorable for black males compared to all other sex-ethnic groups (see Table 2). Black females, however, perform as well as white females.

Using similar Social Security data but a *judgment* sample of trainees and comparison individuals instead of the national sample of Ashenfelter, Kiefer found no net earnings benefits for black males, one, two, and three quarters after training. In contrast, black females made successive quarterly gains of over $200 per quarter. White females had earnings gains that exceeded $100 each of the three quarters but which were substantially less than $200 per quarter.

In short, if we rely more heavily on the Ashenfelter data, which, due to its national scope, is appropriate, we see that adult black males generally gain less than other groups from institutional retraining programs. However, they do gain.

Other Employment/Training Programs: The Supported Work Experiment—The National Supported Work Demonstration is of major value to this discussion because it is a relatively well-managed, mainly on-the-job training and work experience program that incorporates a classical random assignment design. While individuals are randomly assigned into the program, a weakness of the program was the failure to randomly assign individuals to the separate treatments *within* the program. Thus, once in the program, participants could self-select themselves into treatments. So, intertreatment comparisons will contain bias.

In general, large initial program effects were measured across the several target groups of Aid to Families with Dependent Children (AFDC) clients, exaddicts, exoffenders, and youths. Significantly, the postprogram labor market effects for youths disappeared completely sixteen to eighteen months after program enrollment (Maynard et al.). This set of findings then reaffirms the overall judgment that work experience programs may not be effective for youths. However, there are a number of caveats to these findings. First, these are case study results. Second, sample sizes are small and there is a 40 percent nonresponse for the eighteen month data set. The ultimate judgment for these sites and treatments, though, is that they did not significantly benefit the labor market outcomes of the experimental youths, especially since the authors were partly able to account for the nonresponse effect and adjust for it in their benefit estimations.

THE PROBLEM OF DISPLACEMENT

A final major note on all the evaluations discussed above concerns the potential displacement by program participants of other individuals in society. There are several considerations here. First, if program participants displace individuals who are not program eligible, there may be no necessary gain in economic efficiency due to the program. The increase in output of program participants may be cancelled in whole or in part by the lost output of program ineligibles. However, the equity objectives of society can be served by a program with such effects if income is redistributed from higher-income to lower-income individuals. However, if program eligibles are displaced by program participants, neither equity nor efficiency goals are served by the program. Although most of the better studies discussed above mention these concerns and make conjectures concerning the likely direction of effect, none of them actually measures these displacement effects, a task which is admittedly very difficult to do. Thus, this final question about the net social effects of all these programs remains unresolved.

Summary and Conclusions

The results of these few most reliable studies indicate a mixed picture with respect to the effectiveness of employment and training programs for youth. Our efforts to assess these historical programs leave us in considerable uncertainty, mainly because the methods and data used to assess programs have been deficient. But the evidence suggests that, in particular, black youths do not benefit as much as other groups. This is disturbing since this group has been characterized by several studies of the youth unemployment problem as being the most structurally unemployed component. On the other hand, labor market data indicate significant changes in the employment-population ratio of youths as they age. For black males between the ages of sixteen to seventeen and twenty to twenty-four this ratio increases from 19 percent to 62.2 percent. But, this latter figure is to be contrasted with a ratio of 76.8 percent for white males aged twenty to twenty-four. In summary, aging alone improves the employment condition of black males but in no way eliminates their severe disabilities. Wage rates for white and black youths, in contrast, are similar.

Thus, while awaiting the results of improved data and analysis, we are left with the following results, qualified by the fact that most studies are methodologically flawed.

1. Work experience alone does not appear to improve the employability or school attendance of youth, especially for ill-defined jobs with low-level or ill-defined supervision.
2. Work experience may be more effective when combined with other services, including such things as placement services and skill training.

3. Skill training appears to be effective, but its effects decay rather rapidly over time. Some estimates suggest the decay rate may be as high as 15 percent per year. Further, skill training must be specifically linked to known labor market opportunities.

4. Of the services offered youth, other than skill training and work experience, placement services seem to be most effective. Services aimed at changing personal values and personality traits, such as motivation, generally are not successful.

5. Failure to maintain minimum behavioral and program performance standards is self-defeating. Proper management is a necessary condition for an effective program.

6. Success in the workplace is directly related to basic writing, communication, and computational skills.

7. Finally, overall, across the several programs we have discussed *as programs*, the Job Corps, though a relatively small program, exhibits the most reliably reported positive effects. The Youth Incentive Entitlement Pilot Projects program appears at this time to be a promising experiment, but one's optimism here must be tempered by the finding of no effect due to work experience in the supported work experiment.

WHAT IS TO BE DONE?

Several suggestions can be derived from this brief review of youth programs. First, coherent programs with an explicit statement of the program treatment and the expected direction and nature of program effect are desired. In this regard, the Job Corps, the National Supported Work Demonstration, and the Youth Incentive Entitlement Pilot Projects appear to be relatively well-designed and administered.

Second, relative emphasis on the income maintenance or equity aspects of a program to the detriment of the efficiency or human capital-creating aspects may be deleterious to enhancing program effectiveness. This type of strategic error may have been made with the Summer Program for Economically Disadvantaged Youth.

Next, given accurate and timely reporting, the simple equity effects of these programs should first be described, showing the joint distributions by sociodemographic status (target group), program treatments and subtreatments, and direct money outlays. This is the first step required to determine if desired equity effects have been approximated.

Finally, the quality of evaluation and program management must be improved. No program evaluations should be conducted without adjusting for the selection problem. Given program administrators' reluctance to use classical experimental design to test programs, household baseline surveys of program eligibles (and for studies focusing on economy-wide effects, ineligibles) should be mandatory. Due regard should be given to statistically appropriate sample sizes. Definition and collection of data which describe program process are an absolute requirement.

Most studies have been of insufficient sample size due to underfunding and the penchant to scatter small amounts of research funds across a large number of studies. In conclusion, fewer but larger studies should be conducted on a nationwide basis for operating programs.

Bibliography

ASHENFELTER, ORLEY, "What Do Teenage Unemployment Statistics Measure?", in *Supplementary Papers from the Conference on Youth Unemployment: Its Measurement and Meaning*, ed., Naomi Berger Davidson. Washington, D.C.: Employment and Training Administration, U.S. Dept. of Labor, October 1978.

———, "Estimating the Effect of Training Programs on Earnings," *Review of Economics and Statistics* (February 1978).

BARCLAY, SUZANNE, CHRISTINE BOTTOM, GEORGE FARKAS, RANDALL OLSEN, and ERNST W. STROMSDORFER, *Schooling and Work among Youths from Low-Income Households*. New York: Manpower Demonstration Research Corporation, May 1979.

BARTON, PAUL, et al., *The Youth Transition to Work: Synthesis, Research, and Experimentation Strategy, Volume 2, Programs and Experimentation*. Washington, D.C.: Center for Education and Work, National Manpower Institute, March 1978.

CAIN, GLEN G., "Benefit-Cost Estimates for Job Corps." Madison, Wisconsin: Institute for Research on Poverty, University of Wisconsin, 1968.

GENERAL ACCOUNTING OFFICE, COMPTROLLER GENERAL OF THE UNITED STATES, *More Effective Management Is Needed to Improve the Quality of the Summer Youth Employment Program*, HRD-79-45, February 20, 1979.

KIEFER, NICHOLAS M., *The Economic Benefits from Manpower Training Programs* (Technical Analysis Paper #43). Washington, D.C.: Office of

Research and Evaluation, Office of the Assistant Secretary for Policy, Evaluation and Research, U.S. Dept. of Labor, November 1976.

MALLAR, CHARLES, *Evaluation of the Economic Impact of the Job Corps Program: First Follow-up Report.* Washington, D.C.: Office of Program Evaluation, Employment and Training Administration, U.S. Dept. of Labor, December 1978.

MANGUM, GARTH, and JOHN WALSH, *Employment and Training Programs for Youth.* Washington, D.C.: Office of Youth Programs, Employment and Training Administration, U.S. Dept. of Labor, May 1978.

MAYNARD, REBECCA, et al., *The Supported Work Demonstration: Effects During the First 18 Months after Enrollment.* New York: Manpower Demonstration Research Corporation, April 1979.

MOONEY, JOSEPH D., "Teenage Labor Problems and the Neighborhood Youth Corps," in *Critical Issues in Employment Policy,* eds., Frederick H. Harbison and Joseph D. Mooney. Princeton: Industrial Relations Section, Princeton University, 1966.

PERRY, CHARLES R., et al., *The Impact of Government Manpower Programs.* Philadelphia: Industrial Relations Unit, University of Pennsylvania, 1975.

ROBIN, GERALD D., "An Assessment of the In-Public School Neighborhood Youth Corps Project in Cincinnati and Detroit, with Special Reference to Summer Only and Year Round Enrollees." Washington, D.C.: U.S. Dept. of Labor, Manpower Administration, February 1969.

SMITH, ROBERT S., and HUGH M. PITCHER, *The Neighborhood Youth Corps: An Impact Evaluation* (Technical Analysis Paper #9). Washington, D.C.: Office of Evaluation, Office of the Assistant Secretary for Policy Evaluation and Research, U.S. Dept. of Labor, September 1973.

SOMERS, GERALD G., and ERNST W. STROMSDORFER, *A Cost-Effectiveness Study of the In-School and Summer Neighborhood Youth Corps.* Madison, Wisconsin: Industrial Relations Research Institute, University of Wisconsin, 1970.

————, and JENNIFER L. WARLICK, *An Evaluation of Manpower Programs for Young Men, 1964–1972 Based upon the National Longitudinal Surveys.* Washington, D.C.: Office of Research and Development, Employment and Training Administration, U.S. Dept. of Labor, September 1975.

STEVENSON, WAYNE, "The Relationship between Youth Employment and Future Employability and Earnings," in *Supplementary Papers from the Conference on Youth Unemployment: Its Measurement and Meaning,* ed., Naomi Berger Davidson. Washington, D.C.: Employment and Training Administration, U.S. Dept. of Labor, October 1978.

STROMSDORFER, ERNST W., *Review and Synthesis of Cost Effectiveness Studies of Vocational and Technical Education.* Washington, D.C.: Office of Education, Dept. of Health, Education, and Welfare, 1972.

————, KAMRAN MOAYED-DADKHAH, and BRUNO A. OUDET, *An Economic Analysis of the Costs of Selected Manpower Programs.* Washington, D.C.: Office of Policy, Evaluation and Research, U.S. Dept. of Labor, April 1974.

————, and JAMES S. FACKLER, *An Economic and Institutional Analysis of the Cooperative Vocational Education Program in Dayton, Ohio.* Washington, D.C.: Office of Research and Development, Manpower Administration, U.S. Dept. of Labor, August 1973.

TAGGART, ROBERT, III, "Employment and Training Programs for Youth," in *From School to Work: Improving the Transition.* Washington, D.C.: National Commission for Manpower Policy, 1976.

Beatrice G. Reubens

5

Review of Foreign Experience

Most of the industrialized countries have experienced a marked increase in youth unemployment since 1974–75, an increase which has exceeded the rise for other age groups. These countries view their current swollen youth unemployment as different and more serious than previous periods of elevated youth unemployment which temporarily marred the record of full and overfull employment in the 1960s. In that period some countries had even lower unemployment rates for young people than for the labor force as a whole or for prime age (twenty-five to fifty-four) groups. This record is in sharp contrast to the experience over the last two decades in the United States where youth unemployment rates rarely fell below 10 percent.

BEATRICE G. REUBENS, *senior research associate with the Conservation of Human Resources Program at Columbia University and consultant to numerous American and international agencies, is currently completing a comparative study of the youth labor force with the support of the Department of Labor, German Marshall Fund, and Ford Foundation. Under Rockefeller Foundation funding, Dr. Reubens is also directing comparative studies of youth employment, earnings, and unemployment and of youth unemployment programs. John Harrisson gave valuable assistance in the research and writing of this chapter.*

In part because the U.S. has lived with high youth unemployment for so long and in part because employment has grown rapidly even while youth unemployment has remained high, the American view of the current and future situation is less pessimistic than that in many foreign countries. There, recent absolute and relative deterioration in the position of youth appears to be the harbinger of a long period of high youth unemployment. This gloomy assessment arises from a diagnosis which stresses structural factors affecting the youth labor market, the slow growth of many of these economies, the large number expected to enter the labor market in the 1980s, and the small number likely to leave. Not only are the prospects for young people viewed as limited, but stronger fears are expressed about the alienation and radicalization of an entire generation than one hears in the U.S.

Variations in historical experience have created differences between the U.S. and most other nations. One cannot find in foreign countries, as one can in America, a discounting of high overall youth unemployment rates on the grounds that youth unemployment is brief, that rates have not risen much in recent years, and that youth employment/population ratios have increased. Moreover, in other countries, the entire unemployed youth population is the focus of public policy attention. There is nothing abroad which corresponds to the American policy emphasis on minority or poor youth. While certain subgroups in foreign countries have been singled out from the youth unemployed as particularly prone to high incidence or long duration unemployment (children of foreign workers and immigrants, for example) this has occurred within a framework of concern about all unemployed young people. This concern is fostered by the payment of unemployment benefits to young people, whether or not they have previously worked, thus providing a financial incentive to mount public programs.

Unlike the United States, most other countries do not stress the teenage group. They include those from the compulsory school-leaving age of fifteen or sixteen to age twenty-five, with Italy extending the age to thirty. In addition, the inactive youth population in foreign countries—those neither in school nor in the labor force—are, for the most part, not the puzzle or problem they are in the United States. Except for Italy and Canada, countries which also have had persistently high youth unemployment rates, the industrialized countries find that inactive youth constitute a small and explicable proportion of the age group. It is true that in some countries public opinion regards official youth unemployment statistics as inaccurate. However, little interest is shown in replacing traditional measures of unemployment with the U.S. concept of "joblessness" in which the number of unemployed is supplemented by those who are out of school and out of the labor force.

Youth Unemployment Trends

There have been drastic changes in youth unemployment rates in the space of a few years. In the Netherlands, for example, as recently as 1970, the teenage (under nineteen years) male rate was 1.2 percent and the teenage female rate was 0.5 prcent, lower than the rates for the total labor force and very low by any standard. By 1978, the male teenage rate had reached 12.8 percent and the female rate 15.5 percent, compared with total rates of 4.5 percent (male) and 7.7 percent (female). Not only had the teenage rates soared absolutely and relatively by 1978, but teenage females, formerly showing lower rates than comparable males, now surpassed them. This general picture has been typical of several European countries. Standardized data for a number of countries indicate that teenagers have higher rates than young adults (twenty to twenty-four), but the difference in the rates by age varies considerably among countries.

Foreign countries pay more attention to the share of total unemployment represented by young people under twenty-five than does the U.S. Figure 1 shows the absolute numbers of young unemployed and their share of total unemployment from 1969 through 1978, contrasting the situation of the combined European Community (E.C.) membership of nine countries with that of the United States. Such a comparison is reasonable because both the population and labor force for all ages and youth of the E.C. and the U.S. have been roughly of the same magnitude. It is clear that the U.S. has consistently had more unemployed youth than the E.C., even when we count only the U.S. youth not enrolled in school. However, the spread between the U.S. and the E.C. has narrowed perceptibly, especially in the last few years.

Fig. 1. *Numbers of Young People (under 25) Unemployed, and as a Percentage of Total Unemployment, United States and European Economic Community, 1969–1978 (Annual Averages).*

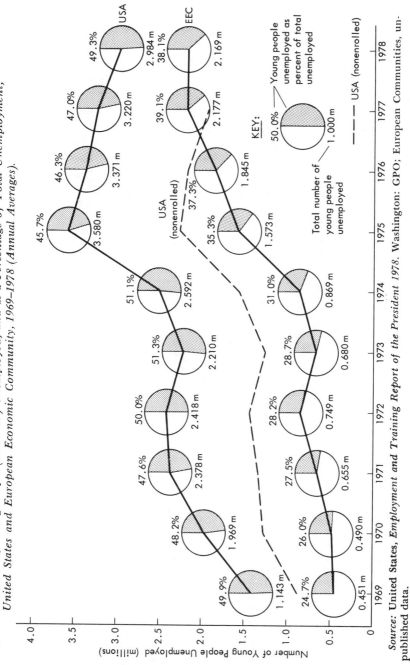

Source: United States, *Employment and Training Report of the President 1978.* Washington: GPO; European Communities, unpublished data.

Even more striking are the differences between the E.C. and the U.S. in the youth share of total unemployment. In the E.C. the upward trend of the share, from 24.7 percent in 1969 to 39.1 percent in 1977, is distinctly associated with an increasing total number of unemployed youth. In other words, youth unemployment rose faster than adult unemployment. In the United States, on the other hand, a rise in the absolute number of unemployed youth has been accompanied by little change in their share of total unemployment (although youth unemployment rates would have risen more than adult rates in absolute terms, as Freeman shows) and vice versa. These differences suggest one reason that the E.C. countries may give a higher relative priority to the youth unemployment problem than is done in the United States.

The changing position of youth also is assessed by comparing the ratios of teenage unemployment rates to prime age adult unemployment rates (Table 1). Seen in this light, American teenage unemployment rates for both sexes were lower in relation to adult rates than in Italy in 1970 and in Italy, France, Sweden, and Aus-

TABLE 1. RATIOS OF TEENAGE TO ADULT UNEMPLOYMENT,
EIGHT COUNTRIES, 1970 & 1977 [1]

	Males		*Females*		*Total*	
	1970	*1977*	*1970*	*1977*	*1970*	*1977*
1. United States	5.4	4.0	3.4	2.9	4.5	3.5
2. Canada	N/A	3.6	N/A	2.2	N/A	2.9
3. Italy [2]	7.6	11.1 [3]	7.2	9.6 [3]	7.4	11.3 [3]
4. France	6.0	7.4 [4]	2.8	4.9 [4]	3.9	6.2 [4]
5. Germany	4.0	2.3	3.4	2.0	4.0	2.2
6. Sweden	3.8	5.3	4.2	4.9	3.9	5.2
7. Australia	6.2	5.6	2.3	4.1	3.9	5.0
8. Japan	3.0	3.6	1.4	1.4	2.2	2.8

Source: U.S. Department of Labor, Bureau of Labor Statistics, *International Comparisons of Unemployment*. Bull. 1979, Table 11. Washington: GPO, 1979; and Supplement.

[1] Ratio of teenage unemployment rate to unemployment rate for persons 25–54 years of age, adjusted to U.S. concepts.

[2] Based on data not adjusted to U.S. concepts.

[3] 1976.

[4] 1975.

tralia in 1977. The ratios of teenage to adult unemployment rates worsened from 1970 to 1977 in Italy, France, Sweden, Japan (males), and Australia (females). Only the United States and Germany showed a relative improvement for young people of each sex. While Wachter's ratios (Table 2) show a downward trend in the U.S., the years cited and the method of calculation are different from those used here. German analysts have challenged official youth unemployment rates, claiming that they would be twice or more as high if the official statistics included certain omitted or undercounted unemployed youth.

Since 1973 the duration of unemployment among young people has lengthened appreciably in several European countries. The continual rise in the proportion of young people with a year or more of unemployment is in sharp contrast to the recent decline in the U.S. in the percentage with six months or more. This difference also may explain the greater emphasis abroad on the whole group of unemployed youth instead of selected subgroups. Compared to the United States, European youth unemployment appears to be concentrated on fewer individuals who undergo relatively longer spells of unemployment.

However, the exclusion from the U.S. data of in-school youth who have relatively short spells (as Wachter has done) might reduce the differences between the U.S. and European countries in which student workers are a negligible or omitted category. In addition, recent analysis of American gross labor force flows suggests that the duration of unemployment spells for youth in the U.S. is artificially shortened by the failure to recognize that time periods classified as "out of the labor force" actually may be extensions of unemployment (Clark and Summers). In that case, the U.S. may have a larger problem of long-duration youth unemployment than has been recognized thus far.

Of particular concern in foreign countries is the new school-leaver whose absorption into employment can be very slow when overall unemployment rises. In some countries, like France and Italy, those seeking a first full-time job constitute over half of the unemployed youth and have an average duration of unemployment in excess of the remainder of the youth group. Accordingly, there are youth programs especially for young people who have never held a job.

The academic low-achiever or the young person without specific occupational skill training or qualifications is singled out frequently in studies of youth unemployment abroad. All countries agree that young people who have not completed compulsory schooling or lack the recognized credentials are at high risk in the labor market; this group corresponds to the U.S. high school dropout. Many now feel that those who merely complete compulsory school and do not obtain additional education or training are a high-risk group.

However, prevailing opinion in various countries does not agree on the relationship between youth unemployment rates and the amount of academic education, especially since some countries now have relatively high rates of unemployment for university graduates. Such nations tend to believe that the value of academic education is exaggerated as a guarantor of immunity from unemployment, although academic education is regarded as important if it provides the qualifications for and leads to specific occupational training, which can reduce the exposure to unemployment. Therefore, few youth programs abroad are directed merely at achieving larger numbers of enrollments and completions in academic or general education, in contrast to the attempts to increase the number who graduate from high school in the U.S.

One exception abroad is the impetus to extend the years of compulsory general education during a period of high youth unemployment or the arrival on the labor market of a baby boom cohort. The extension of compulsory education in Holland and the proposed tenth year of schooling in Germany have been so motivated. But the German states, where jurisdiction over education resides, are generally more interested in using the additional year for vocational preparation than for extending general education. To a greater extent than in the United States, specific occupational skill training is regarded as a preventive against unemployment.

Many countries have a serious minority youth problem, akin to that in the U.S., even though religious and cultural rather than racial differences may be the main issue. One can observe that a Turkish youngster in Germany is treated much the same as a West Indian black in Great Britain. Countries which admitted large numbers of foreign workers on a temporary basis during the labor-short 1960s, expecting that they would return to their homes at the end of the work contract, found instead that many settled in the host country, married locally, or brought wives and children from home. This generation of youngsters were, on the whole, likely to remain in the new country. Whether born abroad or in the host country, they face a less favorable economic climate than their parents and bring more educational and social disadvantages to the labor market than the children of native born parents. Similar problems face many in the generation whose parents were granted citizenship or refugee rights.

It appears that unemployment rates among minority youth abroad are twice or more as high as the rates for the age group as a whole. The relative size of the minority group in other countries is not as large as in the United States, although several countries face the prospect of a sharp rise in the share of the minority population in the total population due to significantly higher birth rates among some of the minorities. But even with lower proportions belonging to minority groups than in the United States, these countries have geographic concentrations of minority populations due to housing patterns and job opportunities, which have created intense local problems with national ramifications. The degree to which minority youth groups abroad are disadvantaged is much the same as for American minority youth. As countries have come to grips with the facts, they have begun to establish special programs, such as bilingual education and remedial courses. However, the American labor market programs directed to minority youth have not yet been widely emulated in other countries, although the E.C. has published reports which praise the American emphasis on disadvantaged youth and urge member countries to follow suit.

Factors in Youth Unemployment

Neither within nor among countries is there a consensus on the causes of youth unemployment. At one extreme are those who relate increasing youth unemployment to overall unemployment trends, finding no youth-specific factors. At the other, are those who emphasize structural factors. In Great Britain, for example, the cyclical explanation has been accepted by both official and academic analysts. However, the Manpower Services Commission, summarizing a series of sponsored surveys, concluded that, in addition to the cyclical explanation there was "also an element resulting from longer-term trends not directly affected by general unemployment levels." Still others in Britain place a heavy stress on structural factors, arguing that cyclical forces are minor.

The more rapid rise of youth than of adult unemployment rates has been a central theme in analyses made in foreign countries, whereas in the United States the concern is to understand a different set of phenomena: the continued high level of youth unemployment rates, the increased concentration of youth unemployment among certain subgroups, and the rise in the proportion of inactive youth (those who are neither in school nor in the labor force). Nevertheless, some of the explanations for high youth unemployment most frequently heard in the United States also appear in other countries. Some of these factors, though not their relative importance, are now discussed.

THE BABY BOOM AND THE YOUTH LABOR FORCE

In relative terms, the baby boom was more intense and prolonged in Australia, New Zealand, and Canada than in the United States. The first two countries welcomed the additional numbers and easily absorbed the baby boom cohorts which entered the labor force in the high growth period of the 1960s. Youth unemployment rates did not rise, although the youth share of the labor force did. But in the 1970s the economic slowdown in these countries resulted in crowding in the youth labor market. Their experience—and that of Japan and the European countries which had shorter and more intense baby booms—indicates that the relationship between demographic trends and youth unemployment varies according to the rate of economic growth. As a consequence, the youth unemployment rate can be higher in a period of relatively small increase in the size of the youth cohort than in a period of larger increase. Because American economic circumstances have not provided the same range of growth rates as in the other countries, analysts in the U.S. have sometimes tended to treat the demographic-unemployment issue as if the relationships were fixed under all economic conditions.

Moreover, analysts who cite only the demographic influences on the youth labor force and omit the effects of trends in educational enrollment may be assuming an increase in the labor supply where in fact there is stability or decline. In several countries, the youth labor supply decreased in spite of an increase in the size of the youth population because educational enrollments in these years were especially high, above the trend. Another factor is the propensity of full time students to work during the school term. This is more highly developed in the U.S. than elsewhere. Because such large proportions of American students work or seek to work and because conventional U.S. labor force statistics count each as a full member of the labor force regardless of how many years they work or seek to work, the United States actually ranked second among twelve industrialized countries in the growth of the teenage labor force from 1950 to 1975. Canada, also a country with many student workers, was in first place. Australia and New Zealand followed the United States, modifying the positions they occupied in terms of demographic trends. The propensity of American in-school youth to seek work therefore appears to be more important as a comparative supply side factor than the demographic trend itself. Much of the employment gain for U.S. youth has been among students, who, as part-time workers, tend to have lower wage rates than full-time youth, and thus depress the level of youth earnings relative to adult.

COMPETITION BETWEEN YOUTH AND OLDER WOMEN

Would employers hire more youth if they did not have the option of employing adult women? The issue is the extent to which the two groups are good substitutes for one another in various jobs and the preferences of employers in countries where this is the case. British surveys of employers who had recently hired sixteen to eighteen year olds indicate that, in about 40 percent of their jobs, women were considered in competition with young people. If applicants of broadly similar qualifications were available, 42 percent of the employers had no preference between the two categories, but 40 percent preferred women to young people, and many were willing to take women without previous work experience. Similar indications that mature women may be taking jobs that otherwise would have gone to young people, especially girls, have been noted in Sweden, Canada, and Australia, all countries in which female labor force participation rates have risen markedly. Coupled with expressions of preference for mature women, even if inexperienced, are explicit employer complaints about the attitudes, behavior, appearance, and social skills of the young people whom they interview.

Whatever preference employers may express for women workers instead of young people, it has not prevented adult women in most industrialized countries from experiencing substantial increases in unemployment rates; the loss of jobs may have been largely in occupations where young people are hardly employed. In some countries public policy has shifted from concern about unemployed youth to adult women or at least from male youth to all females including those under twenty-five.

LEGAL MINIMUM WAGE

In the United States there is a strong belief that the introduction of a youth differential in the legal minimum wage would lower employer costs, increase youth employment, and decrease unemployment. Only a few of the industrialized nations have enacted statutory minimum wage rates while several others achieve effective legal minimums in specific occupations or industries through the generalization of collective bargaining agreements and similar methods. Of those having legal minimums, youth differentials are provided by the Netherlands, France, and Portugal at the national level and by Canada's provinces and Japan's prefectures (separately for different industries and occupations).

Canadian youth differentials in the minimum wage were established as early as 1919 in British Columbia. They existed in some form in all provinces and territories by 1968. Three provinces, Saskatchewan, New Brunswick, and Newfoundland, and the Yukon territory abolished the youth differential in recent years for reasons which are not readily available from official sources in Ottawa. Nor is evidence available about the subsequent effects on youth employment. A federal youth minimum wage was introduced in 1965, covering a small number of workers in industries under federal jurisdiction.

Provincial legislation often distinguishes between student workers and others, or singles out particular types of youth jobs for special treatment. Local differences in minimums also exist within some provinces. While provincial minimum wage provisions exclude some industries, such as agriculture, most workers in traditionally low-paid industries are covered. Canadian youth minimum wages, identical for males and females, have an upper age limit of seventeen or eighteen, since adult rates begin at eighteen. With the school-leaving age set at sixteen in most provinces and considerable voluntary prolongation of education, the chief effect of the youth differential appears to be on student workers. There are no incremental steps in the youth rate according to age, and the differential between youth and adult minimum wage rates is small, currently ranging from 5 percent in Alberta to 13 percent in the Northwest Territories.

It may be these aspects of the Canadian youth differential which have failed to make it an important force in holding down the high youth unemployment rates. Whether youth unemployment might have been still higher in the absence of a youth minimum is difficult to say. When British Columbia increased the differential between adult and youth minimum wages, making young people more attractive to employers, an increase in employment of those under eighteen occurred, but it is not known whether it was at the expense of older workers. Surveys at the end of the 1960s among provincial officials suggested that the minimum wage differential was a positive factor in introducing young people into working life. Other provincial officials believe that the youth differential caused displacement of older workers and that some youth were laid off once they attained the adult rate. Trade union leaders were generally unenthusiastic about the youth minimum wage, doubting its use in introducing young people to working life and holding that it depressed wage levels. However, several observers noted that the differential was ineffective since youth often were offered the same rates as adults, and in economically buoyant periods employers found that they had to pay above the youth minimum to attract labor.

The Netherlands' minimum wage law of 1966 was changed in 1974 to introduce a legal youth differential, based on the age differentials in 1973 collective bargaining agreements. The monthly minimum wage of fifteen year olds is set at 40 percent of the twenty-three year old (adult) level, and at each successive year of age the proportion rises, reaching 55 percent at seventeen years, 70 percent at nineteen years, and 85 percent at twenty-one years. These newly-established ratios of minimum wages for youth were lower than actual 1973 youth wages in the industrial sector. The relationship in other sectors was not clear, but the law may have increased youth labor costs in some fields. Moreover, a particular problem was created by the failure to make separate provision for apprentice wages, traditionally much lower than those of young workers. Apprentices now receive the minimum applicable wage, and employers state that the increased cost is a deterrent to offering apprenticeships. Finally, the minimum wage level for adults rose rapidly, doubling from 1971 to 1976 and increasing by another 43 percent by 1979. Since the youth-to-adult wage ratios are fixed, youth minimum wages have also risen sharply.

While these specific problems are unlikely to appear in an American youth differential, the Dutch experience underlines the importance of carefully working out the details of a youth differential, paying attention to its level, geographic variability, and its rate of change. Charges are made in Holland that the legal imposition of a youth differential is partly responsible for the surge in youth unemployment beginning in 1975. This argument has been met officially by reference to the soaring youth unemployment rates in countries which have no legal regulation of youth wages.

In France, the legal minimum wage, established in 1950, sets the adult level which is reached at eighteen years. It is reduced by 10 percent for seventeen to eighteen year olds, 20 percent for those under seventeen, and even more for starting apprentices. Complaints are not raised about the youth differentials or the legal minimum wage itself, perhaps because a small part of the labor force is affected. Portugal's law of 1975 guarantees teenagers 50 percent of the adult minimum, but enforcement has lagged and its effects are not known.

RELATIVE WAGE LEVELS AND TRAINING COSTS

Reduced differentials in earnings between young and older workers have been observed in several countries (contrary to the findings for the U.S. by Freeman and Wachter). Training costs are relatively high for new entrants, and in some countries the ratio of so-cial security charges to the wages of young people is also high. Thus, it has been suggested that employers prefer other age groups and that the productivity of some young people does not equal the costs of employing them. Hard evidence is difficult to find. In Great Britain where the erosion of pay differentials by age has been attributed to "flat rate" pay settlements and the lowering of the age for receipt of the adult rate of pay, surveys among employers have not shown the issue to be important in the recruitment of young people. Over four-fifths of the firms which had hired a young person in 1976 said that their hiring policy was not affected by the reduction in the age for the full adult wage rate.

The possibility that the actual levels of youth earnings plus fringe benefits and training costs may be as much of an obstacle to additional youth employment as the legal minimum wage should be considered when the youth differential is urged as a panacea. A broader view of wage and other rigidities in the labor market suggests that the U.S. should not pin excessive hopes on the bene-fits of a youth differential in the minimum wage.

INCOME TRANSFERS

Unlike the U.S., most other industrialized countries offer young people, even those who have never worked before, some sort of payment while they are unemployed. These payments are poten-tially greater disincentives, both in terms of relative numbers af-fected and the nature of the payments, than are the income transfers directly or indirectly available to American youth, referred to by Freeman and Wachter. Popular opinion in most countries, but especially in Holland and Belgium, holds that youth unemploy-ment has been increased by such unemployment benefits. The case in Belgium is particularly strong because once the seventy-five-day waiting period has been completed, benefits are of unlimited dura-tion. A Dutch study of school-leavers found some prolongation of unemployment due to receipt of benefits, but considered that the longer search period might have produced superior jobs. British investigations suggest little or no effect on youth unemployment due to receipt of unemployment benefits or means-tested supplementary benefits, available at age sixteen.

JOB CHANGING

One of the common explanations of the high ratio of youth to adult unemployment rates in the United States is the high rate of job changing, especially voluntary job leaving by young people. Some light is thrown on the subject by a British longitudinal study of young people who changed jobs frequently, on average, more than once every six months. Although the group constituted only about 3 percent of the age group, it accounted for a high proportion of the age group's job changing and as much as 50 percent of youth unemployment when such rates were low, falling to as little as 10 percent when youth unemployment was very high. The frequent job changers did not leave voluntarily in almost half the cases, but were fired. Dismissal for disciplinary reasons played a large role, as did arguments with employers or supervisors and refusal to do certain menial tasks. The chronic job changers tended to get jobs requiring lower skills as they moved from job to job. Heavily concentrated in occupations and industries with high turnover rates, the chronic job changers gave every indication of being confined to a secondary youth labor market. As the group aged, its rate of job changing slowed considerably, although not to the levels of the remainder of the age group. These patterns for white British youth are similar to American findings for inner-city youth, as Elijah Anderson graphically describes. This group which contributed so disproportionately to British youth unemployment was said to need the special services of a variety of public agencies. Similar studies are needed in the U.S. of chronic job changers, their educational, socio-economic, and racial composition, their reasons for losing or leaving jobs, their occupational progress over the years, and their share of youth unemployment.

Beyond the specific causes discussed above, the factors most commonly cited in national discussions of youth unemployment are an educational/labor market mismatch, an aspirations/job mismatch, legal restrictions such as in child labor laws, inadequate preparation for the work world, poor occupational and labor market information and inefficient job search techniques, the increased job security granted established workers, and relative or absolute declines in the types of employment teenagers are likely to enter as their initial full-time jobs.

Youth Unemployment Programs

The measures adopted by countries to deal with unemployed youth are limited in number and can be classified under the dozen types listed in Table 2.

Without copying directly from one another, countries arrive at the same list of alternatives. There are few programs that are novel or unknown elsewhere. On the contrary, the absence of dramatic new approaches to youth unemployment is the most conspicuous feature of the widespread efforts in the 1970s. What does vary among countries is the size of the effort, the type of youth pro-

TABLE 2. NEW AND REINFORCED NATIONAL PROGRAMS TO COUNTER YOUTH UNEMPLOYMENT, 17 OECD COUNTRIES, 1975–78 [1]

Type of Program	Number of Countries
Private Sector [2]	
Employment	10
Employment with training (including apprenticeship)	14
Training (including off-the-job training)	8
Work experience	7
Public Sector	
Job creation (including community work)	15
Training, preapprenticeship	10
Basic education	7
Advanced education	2
Transition from school to work (may include training)	6
Information and vocational guidance	11
Placement service	3
Mobility	2

Source: Reports of International Agencies and National Governments.

[1] Excludes the United States. Programs counted only once, if they were renewed or extended with the same basic elements. Includes some programs not exclusively for young people, but mainly serving youth. Some countries have more than one program under a given category, but are counted once only.

[2] May apply also in public enterprises and the public sector.

grams, their details and special features, their permanence, the target populations, the administrative structures, the costs, and the priority given to youth programs over others.

Within this framework of similarity among countries, some distinctive patterns emerge. After some experimentation with a number of separate programs, Britain decided on a single Youth Opportunities Program, comprising a variety of public and private sector work experience, education, and training possibilities, but excluding on-the-job training or direct employment. In contrast, French programs have been heavily directed toward subsidizing increased employment and training opportunities in the private sector, while Germany has relied on an expansion of apprenticeships under the threat of a tax on employers and reduced employer control over the apprenticeship system.

Countries have shown similarities in the increased attention given in periods of rising youth unemployment to improving the preparation of young people for the world of work and easing the transition from school to work. Special measures along these lines have been instituted to aid unemployed youth who are not in direct employment or training programs. In addition, more basic changes are contemplated in the educational and occupational information and guidance-placement systems, as well as in the nature of youth jobs, in order to reduce the risk of unemployment for those who have not yet entered the work world. Specific programs that are noteworthy include the Danish and Swedish outreach systems in which every school-leaver, not in education, training, or employment, is personally followed up and offered assistance; the British Unified Vocational Preparation Scheme, designed to give employed young people who enter jobs without training or advancement possibilities additional training and education as a part of their jobs; and the French proposals to make a period of work in an enterprise a normal part of education at all levels. These are only a few examples of innovative measures.

Major differences between the U.S. and other countries should be noted in the provision for unemployed young people. The most significant difference is the emphasis in some foreign countries on establishing a network of programs to assure every unemployed young person either a job or a place in a training or educational setting. This commitment has been explicitly adopted in the Scandinavian countries, Great Britain, and the Netherlands. Germany hopes to provide occupational training, on or off-the-job, to all young people. In the view of the Dutch government, it is important also to provide community activities which make young people feel like functioning members of society, combating the alienation which otherwise threatens.

To be sure, the realization of these quantitative goals lies in the future, and questions remain about the qualitative aspects of some of the programs. But the declarations of national intent are significant. It can be argued that the motivation to offer such guarantees is stronger in other countries than it is in the United States, since those countries pay benefits of some sort to unemployed young people, even if they have never worked. Therefore, active programs for employment, training, or education can be mounted for little additional budgetary cost. Also, other countries do not feel as much pressure as is found in the U.S. to concentrate resources on the subgroups of youth with the most serious unemployment problems.

Another point of difference is the greater utilization through wage subsidies and government allowances of the private sector in European youth programs. The degree of use of the private sector is not uniform in the European countries, but, on the whole it is greater than in the United States. Table 2 shows, for seventeen Organization for Economic Cooperation and Development (OECD) countries, excluding the United States, the numbers of countries which have various types of youth programs at the national level. It appears that private sector programs offering employment with training, including apprenticeships, are the most popular, but programs providing employment alone or training alone (including off-the-job apprenticeships) or work experience are well represented.

The scale, form, and coverage of the wage subsidies to employers in foreign countries appear to be determined fairly arbitrarily. Such programs have proved most popular with small firms and tend to be concentrated in the service sector, especially retail distribution, rather than in manufacturing. Commonly, the youth employment created by wage subsidies is of a labor-intensive nature, in low-paid, high-turnover occupations.

In the public sector, job creation programs which are exclusively or mainly for young people appear in almost all of the countries. Training programs, including occupational preparation for apprenticeship, are also prominent. Basic or remedial education and transitional courses are another response to the increase in youth unemployment. While all countries have had some form of public information, guidance, and placement activity for young people, eleven of the seventeen countries reinforced or added new information and/or guidance programs during the period of increased youth unemployment. Stimulation of geographical mobility, as a special youth program, plays a minor role.

In countries with a federal government, youth programs may be initiated at the state, regional, or local level as well. Germany, Canada, and Australia have many youth programs which operate independently of the federal government, although they may be designed to supplement or fill gaps in federal programs. They are not counted in Table 2.

Young people also are served by programs without age restrictions. In some cases these general programs enroll more young people than the special youth programs. Also, youth may be represented more than any other age group, or a disproportionate share may be represented in terms of the youth share of unemployment. For example, almost one-third of those affected by the German wage subsidy in 1974–75 were under twenty-five, although the group constituted just over one-fifth of the unemployed at the time. In Britain, the Temporary Employment Subsidy, an all-age program, is one of the largest of all the programs. The youth share (under twenty-five years) of 23 percent might have involved as many or more young people than the total in all specific youth programs. However, with the exception of job creation programs, Table 2 reports only youth-oriented programs.

Since participants in most employment programs are not counted as unemployed, it is useful to compare the number of young people in such programs with the residual number unemployed and the total number in the age group (Table 3). It is clear that the youth unemployment programs engage only a very small proportion of the age group, with little spread among the countries. Even the introduction of a narrower age band for the population, more in keeping with the actual age distribution in the youth programs, would not raise the percentage significantly.

Potential unemployment may be said to be reduced by the number engaged in programs. Conceptually and practically there are

TABLE 3. NUMBER IN YOUTH UNEMPLOYMENT PROGRAMS AND TOTAL
NUMBER OF YOUTH UNEMPLOYED, FIVE COUNTRIES, 1975-79

Country	Total Number Unemployed [1] (14–24)	Percent Females in Unemployed	Total Number in Programs	Percent Females in Programs	Total in Programs as Percent of Population [1] (14–24)
	(000s)	(Percent)	(000s)	(Percent)	(Percent)
Belgium	77	68	56 [2]	43	0.03
France	419	61	546 [3]	42	0.07
Great Britain	335 [4]	44	140 [5]	40	0.02 [7]
			(187) [6]	N/A	
Ireland	41	32	10 [8]	N/A	0.02
Netherlands	52	42	128 [9]	58	0.05

Sources: European Communities. *Labour Force Sample Survey, 1977.* Luxembourg: Eurostat, 1978, and national and international official reports.

[1] 1977 data from E.C. Labour Force Sample Survey.

[2] 1977–78 data.

[3] February 1978 data. Consists of stocks and flows.

[4] E.C. survey data for United Kingdom adjusted to G.B. base from national data.

[5] 1976–77 data.

[6] 1978–79 (estimate).

[7] E.C. survey population data for United Kingdom adjusted to G.B. base from other survey tables.

[8] 1976–78 data.

[9] 1975–78 data. Figure includes 99,000 in minimum wage subsidy scheme, an indirect unemployment program.

Timing of unemployment data and information on youth programs does not necessarily coincide. Number of youth program participants is derived from stock data on a variety of dates or a combination of stocks and flows. Data on numbers of youth in all-age programs are incomplete and inadequate and are not included, although these programs may be numerically highly significant for youth. Finally, the countries shown may be at different points in their business cycles and program development.

difficulties with such calculations, especially across nations. It is possible that programs also enlarge the youth labor force, drawing on some who were not previously unemployed. Some programs continue to count participants as unemployed. Belgium, for example, in its public service job creation, regards all participants as unemployed and available for regular jobs.

In France the real reduction in the unemployment register is judged to be 80 to 100 thousand, after allowing for the unregistered unemployed in the program, the substitution of subsidized youth for others who become unemployed, and the displacement of other age groups by subsidized youth. Table 3 also indicates that, based on partial returns, females were underrepresented in programs in Belgium and France and overrepresented in the Netherlands. In general, experts believe that youth programs cater too heavily to males.

Evaluation of Programs

Compared to American practice, the evaluation of youth programs in most other countries has been infrequent, unsystematic, and often methodologically dubious. However, European countries are more likely than the U.S. to ask the young people what they think of the programs in which they participate and to use these responses in judging the programs.

Academically acceptable evaluations exist for a few programs. Under OECD auspices, an evaluation was made of the French "Pacte National" of July 1977 which established a set of youth programs, mainly in the private sector. The evaluation found only limited effects on net new job creation, but because of the difficulty of distinguishing between hiring which might have occurred in any case, hiring which was speeded up because of subsidies, and hiring which would not have occurred at all, hard numbers on job creations were not offered. Nor do the available data allow a conclusion to be drawn about an age redistribution of unemployment as a result of the youth programs.

Some unintended and possibly permanent labor market effects of the temporary programs are noted: that management may come to regard the entire category of young people as marginal and only to be hired with subsidies; that youth job instability may be increased by programs which permit employers to avoid offering a work contract for the initial employment period; and that seasonal fluctuations in the recruitment of young people would be intensified because programs are seasonally oriented.

The estimated macroeconomic effects of the programs in 1978 showed small increases in consumption by households, gross domestic production, and overall demand, no decrease in prices, and a modest increase in the trade deficit. French policy makers, as well as those in Sweden and other countries, remain convinced that wage and training subsidies have a useful place in youth unemployment programs.

British evaluations of two youth wage subsidy programs—the Recruitment Subsidy for School-leavers and its successor, the Youth Employment Subsidy—led to the abandonment of the programs. A change in the eligibility requirements which targeted on youth with longer-duration unemployment did not remove the basic weakness—that the wage subsidy resulted in a very small net increase in hiring during the period of subsidy and possibly a reduction thereafter. Employers hired young people they would have recruited without a subsidy, substituted subsidized for unsubsidized youth, and to a small degree, took young people instead of older workers.

The British Work Experience Program (WEP), a predecessor of the current Youth Opportunities Program, was targeted on unemployed low academic achievers among sixteen to eighteen year olds and designed to assist in the transition from school to work. In order to obtain acceptance by the trade unions, the program participants were not to engage in the firms' productive processes, thus avoiding the displacement of regular employees. In practice, some contributions to productive output probably occurred. A survey of employer sponsors showed that 13 percent felt the program had persuaded them to hire more young people, while 1 percent said they would employ fewer. Effectively, 20 percent of the recruitment to the program resulted in the unemployment of other young people and adults. In the long run there is estimated to be a net employment increase of 13 to 16 percent for youth and a net decrease for adults of 6 to 9 percent. WEP was judged more favorable than general reflation in its effects on the balance of payments, the public sector borrowing requirements, the financial requirements of the business sector, and the distribution of income. It was less favorable in its effect on employment (defined as the number of jobs created per £100 million net public expenditure), the growth of Gross Domestic Product, and the likely efficiency of enterprises.

Although the Youth Opportunities Program (YOP), which caters to registered unemployed youth, is too new to be evaluated properly, an early assessment concluded that the program was about 85 percent effective in reducing registered unemployment. The remainder reflects those young people or adults who were replaced or not hired as a result of the program's operations. Like the WEP, YOP is also favorable compared to general reflation in its effect on the balance of payments, public sector borrowing requirements, and distributional patterns and on the grounds of timing, flexibility, and control. On balance it may be favorable in relation to the easing of supply constraints and the financial position of the business sector, but is less favorable in its effect on Gross Domestic Product and microefficiency within firms.

Many additional country analyses of the costs and benefits of youth programs are required, using comparable data, concepts, and methodology, if the effectiveness of programs and program-mixes is to be evaluated across nations. A broader view of how these temporary youth programs might be evaluated is offered by Dutch officials. Taking the position that the long-term effects of such measures are difficult to assess, they approve them as short-term measures on the grounds that they prevent the undesirable effects of unemployment from falling exclusively or heavily on weaker groups in the labor market. But, at the same time, they call for long-run macroeconomic policies combined with active labor market policy to adjust demand and supply to one another.

The present situation in most of the countries surveyed suggests that the temporary youth programs have had a reasonable degree of official and public acceptance. In many cases, the former year-to-year extension of measures has been replaced by a commitment for a longer time period. The British Youth Opportunities Program, for example, was given a five-year life, and it may form the basis for a permanent program which could even be extended to certain employed youth as well, although the recent change of government may alter earlier plans.

A significant development of the past few years has been the establishment of closer working relationships between the employment and education authorities in various countries as they strive to meet the goal of furnishing all out-of-school teenagers (or certain age groups) with a useful activity—a job or an educational place or a training opportunity. In the process, there has been much cooperative activity toward improving the educational process, the preparation of all young people for work, and the transition from school to work.

Recognizing that an expansion of the total number of employment opportunities is a basic need and seeing few chances of significant employment growth on the medium-run future, several European countries have turned to proposals for work sharing, reduced work hours, early retirement plans, and related programs. It is unlikely that these approaches will win much favor in the U.S. If there is any single aspect of foreign youth unemployment programs which might be cited for serious consideration in America, it would be the adoption, as a part of national policy, of the goal of leaving no unemployed teenager without a public offer of employment, education, or training. Coupled with the type of outreach and follow-up programs initiated in Denmark and Sweden, such a program would indeed represent a new direction and scope for American policy.

Bibliography

BAILY, M., and J. TOBIN, "The Macroeconomic Effects of Selective Public Employment and Wage Subsidies," *Brookings Papers on Economic Activity* (2: 1977).

BAXTER, J. L., "The Chronic Job Changer: A Study of Youth Employment," *Social and Economic Administration* (Autumn 1975).

CLARK, K. B., and L. H. SUMMERS, *The Dynamics of Youth Unemployment* (Working Paper no. 274). Cambridge: National Bureau of Economic Research, 1978.

GRUBEL, H. G., and M. A. WALKER, eds., *Unemployment Insurance: Global Evidence of its Effects on Unemployment.* Vancouver, B.C.: The Frazer Institute, 1978.

MAKEHAM, P., "The Young and Out-of-Work," Department of Employment *Gazette* (August 1978).

MUKHERJEE, S., *There's Work to be Done.* London: Manpower Services Commission, 1974.

PALMER, J., ed., *Creating Jobs: Public Employment Programs and Wage Subsidies.* Washington: Brookings Institution, 1978.

RHODES, F. A., *A Study of the Impact of Minimum Wage Revisions on Selected Business Establishments in British Columbia.* British Columbia: Department of Labor, Research Branch, 1973.

SCHMID, G., "The Impact of Selective Employment Policy: The Case of a Wage-Cost Subsidy Scheme in Germany 1974–75," *Journal of Industrial Economics* (March 1979).

Bernard E. Anderson and
Isabel V. Sawhill

6

Policy Approaches for the Years Ahead

Introduction

High and rising rates of youth unemployment have attracted national, and indeed international, attention. In the United States, an unemployment rate in the neighborhood of 12 percent for those sixteen to twenty-four years of age, together with a large and growing gap between the labor market prospects of white and minority youth, have intensified efforts to understand and respond to the problem. In fact, these statistics appear to have taken on a political life of their own and have become a powerful weapon in the hands of those who advocate a greater commitment of resources to the nation's youth.

Concern about youth unemployment has not been limited to the United States. At the economic summit meeting in London in May of 1977, the leaders of the major Western countries flagged the issue as a critical common problem. Their discussions led to the convening of a ministerial level OECD conference in December of 1977, under the chairmanship of U.S. Secretary of Labor Ray Marshall. The resulting communiqué noted that all unemployment is wasteful, but that "youth unemployment has particular human,

social, and economic consequences because of the important role
to be played by the younger generation in the future development
of our countries."

In the United States, a commitment to respond to the problem
was embodied in bipartisan support for new legislation signed into
law on August 5, 1977. The Youth Employment and Demonstration
Projects Act (YEDPA) created four new youth programs serving
approximately 200,000 youth annually at a cost of about one billion
dollars. (These program funds are in addition to the one billion
dollars or more being spent on the Job Corps and the Summer
Youth Employment Program.) Two features of this legislation are
particularly noteworthy. First, it was heavily targeted on "disadvantaged" youth, i.e., those from low-income families. Second, it
was recognized that the causes of youth unemployment, and the
best ways of reducing it, are not well understood. Consequently,
YEDPA was structured to allow experimentation with a number of
different approaches, and a strong research or "knowledge development" component was built into the law. Unfortunately, very little
of this new knowledge became available before the legislation ex-
piration on September 30, 1980.

In 1979, the Carter Administration engaged in a major effort
to review youth employment policies in order to recommend some
new initiatives. Concern about the problem was expressed by both
Democratic and Republican members of the Congress, by both business and labor, as well as by civil rights leaders and a broad spectrum of the American public. In short, there appears to be little
disagreement about the importance of the issue, but a good deal
of uncertainty about how best to respond. One clear danger is
that resources will be committed to "solving the problem," but that
they will be ineffective in accomplishing their objectives, leading
to the kind of neoconservative backlash which has plagued so much
of the social legislation of the 1960s. Political realities almost always
demand that objectives be ambitiously, if sometimes rhetorically,
defined and that action be taken sooner rather than later. But
experience suggests that there are no simple cures for difficult social
problems. Failure will be almost inevitable if too much is expected
too soon and if new efforts are undertaken before the nature and
dimension of the problem are more clearly understood.

It is appropriate, then, to ask some tough questions about where public policies designed to deal with youth unemployment should be headed. Is the current expenditure of about $2.2 billion for special youth employment and training programs sufficient? Should they be reallocated or merged into regular CETA programs which also serve large numbers of young people? Is there any way to utilize over $100 billion worth of expenditures on education (largely state and local funds) more effectively to improve the employment prospects of young people without undermining other educational objectives? What form should any new efforts take, and can existing programs of general education, vocational education, training, and employment be better coordinated?

Table 1 provides an overview of 1979 and 1980 federal expenditures on employment and training programs for youth. In thinking about new directions for policy, it is well to bear in mind that budget resources are limited, and that the era of rapidly expanding expenditures for social programs may have come to an end. In this context, devoting more resources to youth employment and training programs implies devoting less to other, more adult-oriented programs and raises philosophical conundrums about how much priority should be given to youth and what the scale of any new effort should be. We live in a society in which every group, with the possible exception of adult white males, has come to expect special governmental assistance. Each group presses its claims in relative isolation from the others, and few seem to be willing to face up to the difficult trade-offs which these competing claims entail. At present, a high proportion of those in the labor force are members of a group which has been designated as deserving special assistance under various employment-related programs. For example, minorities, women, and older workers comprise 69 percent of the labor force. Adding sixteen to twenty-one year old white males would increase the size of this group to 76 percent of the labor force. Clearly, some finer distinctions about who should be the focus of concern, or the target groups for any new federal assistance, must be made. We need to ask: should priority be given to youth over adult workers, and, within the youth population, who should be served?

In the final analysis, these decisions will, and should, be made in the political arena, but there are a number of criteria and certain facts which may illuminate the debate. First and foremost, it

TABLE 1. OVERVIEW OF YOUTH PROGRAMS

($ in Millions)

	1979			1980		
	Budgetary Authority	Outlays	Average Slots	Budgetary Authority	Outlays	Average Slots
Youth Employment and Demonstration Projects Act (YEDPA) total	$ 931	$1,186	194,100	$1,098	$1,186	203,700
—Young Adult Conservation Corps	217	307	29,200	166	153	14,600
—Youth Community Conservation and Improvement Projects	107	140	17,400	134	140	16,600
—Youth Incentive Entitlement Pilot Projects	107	148	28,000	—	43	7,700
—Youth Employment and Training Programs	500	592	119,500	798	850	164,800
Job Corps	296	375	30,300	416	400	42,000
Summer Program for Economically Disadvantaged Youth (SPEDY)	740	681	1,000,000 [1]	411	545	750,000 [1]
Total youth programs	$1,967	$2,243		$1,925	$2,131	

Source: U.S. Department of Labor.
[1] Represents number of opportunities provided during the summer months.

seems reasonable to inquire about the significance of joblessness for youth relative to adults.

The Consequences of Youth Unemployment

All involuntary joblessness represents a loss of real output for society as well as a loss of income for the individual. These losses are likely to be more serious in the case of an adult than in the case of a teenager. Adults are generally more experienced and productive and are also more likely to have family responsibilities. Offsetting this is the fact that teenagers and young adults who cannot find work may be more inclined to engage in antisocial behavior. Although the links between youth unemployment and such phenomena as crime, teenage pregnancy, and social alienation are not that well established in a *causal* sense, common sense and observation have clearly refuted the hypothesis of "no relationship" in the popular mind. Finally, a preference for treating youth over adult unemployment may stem from the belief that this represents an investment in the next generation. Put most simply, today's young people will become tomorrow's adults. And failure to obtain employment experiences and knowledge of the world of work while young *may* have long-term deleterious effects. These so called "scarring effects" can take the form of less stable employment, lower earnings, withdrawal from the labor force, or even some psychological impairment as an adult.

Data from the National Longitudinal Survey which follows the same individuals over time provide some evidence on these long-term effects. Studies indicate that a period of unemployment while in school does not appear to have any very long-lasting effects. On the other hand, being out of school *and* out of work as an adolescent or young adult is more clearly related to later labor market problems. Specifically, joblessness in the period immediately after leaving school is associated with lower wages a few years later, even after adjusting for individual differences which simultaneously explain both early and later success in the labor market. Whether it is the acquisition of good work habits, specific job training, a network of job contacts, or the credentialing effect of a prior work record which explains the relationship between early labor market experience and subsequent wages is not entirely clear; but probably all play a part.

To summarize, although youth are generally less productive than adults, and often have less immediate need for income, providing them with employment experiences may have a favorable impact on their later economic success, with potentially long-lasting benefits for both the individuals and society. While these arguments provide no firm basis for allocating resources between different age groups, they suggest some of the reasons why youth might be given special attention in employment and training programs. In 1978, of the 3.9 million program participants in training and employment-related activities, 34 percent were youth (between the ages of fourteen and twenty-two). This same age group represented 15 percent of the entire U.S. population, 26 percent of the poverty population, and 40 percent of those who were unemployed.

Policy Objectives

Even more important than the question of whether the employment of youth should be a national priority is the issue of who should be served *within* the youth population and what the objectives of any new initiatives should be. Although there is a tendency for all social programs to have ill-defined or multiple objectives, making it difficult to establish any agreed upon performance standards, employment and training programs have been particularly hard to evaluate for this reason. Any new set of policies needs to be built on a firmer understanding of the *nature* of the problem, of *what* it is we are trying to accomplish, and *for whom?*

First, it is important to recognize that employment may not be the ultimate, or only, objective for youth. Not long ago society felt compelled to pass laws restricting the employment of children and making school attendance universal and compulsory up to a certain age. While the pendulum may now have swung too far in the direction of prolonging childhood and the educational experiences of youth, surely we feel differently about jobs for fourteen year olds than we do for those who are beyond high school age. And to the extent that we seek to create employment opportunities for adolescents, it may be mainly in the spirit of providing some practical education and exposure to the adult world of work and its values.

What is the appropriate balance between jobs and education, between employment and employability? And how can they be more effectively combined at different ages? Probably there is an implicit model of human development in most people's minds, one which emphasizes learning during childhood and productive work during adulthood but with a good deal of overlap between the two at any age and a lengthy period during which each individual makes the transition from one to the other. Our institutions have sometimes failed to recognize the need for this transition to occur gradually rather than abruptly. Schools have tended to overspecialize in traditional teaching and learning activities while employers have tended to neglect them in favor of immediate productivity. These different emphases are to be expected, given the very different missions of these institutions. However, some thought might be given to whether new incentives could be created which would realign the behavior of both schools and employers to make them more congruent with the developmental needs of adolescents.

For school-age youth greater emphasis might be placed on linking their education with actual work experience. However, the value of such work experience will depend upon how it is structured, what kind of supervision and learning experiences are provided, and the different learning styles and needs of the youth themselves. In some cases, employment can complement and enhance the value of education in preparing young people for productive roles. In others, it may compete in an unhealthy fashion with the acquisition of basic skills which have greater long-term payoffs. While it has often been assumed that work opportunities will permit students to stay in school, thus far no credible study has ever demonstrated a relationship between the two, and analyses of why students drop out of high school suggest that educational and personal reasons are more important than the lack of money. Additional evidence on this issue will eventually be provided by the experience with a job guarantee for in-school, low-income youth under YEDPA. This experience is being carefully monitored to see whether entitlement to a job increases school retention rates. Beyond this, there is a growing concern about the tendency of the educational establishment to force every school-age youth into the same academic mold. With a higher proportion of the population attending high school than in the past, some argue that we should be providing more educational options including more experiential learning or cooperative work-education programs to meet the needs of a diverse group of students. However, these options are clearly oriented toward long-term employability or preparation for adult roles, not simply short-term needs for income.

As adolescents move toward, and then beyond, the normal school-leaving age—say eighteen for noncollege bound youth—employment gradually takes on a new meaning as a source of both income and status for the individual and his or her family. At this point, it may be more appropriate to emphasize access to relatively permanent jobs, four-fifths of which are in the private sector. Access to these jobs will depend, in part, on previous preparation for work, on the willingness of employers to provide additional training or socialization to what they often perceive as a relatively high-risk group, and on the availability of jobs where youth reside.

Youth Most at Risk

Whether one wishes to stress preparation for work while in school or access to jobs later on, it is clear that not all youth are equally at risk. As indicated in previous chapters, many young people make the transition to adult roles quite successfully. We have seen that a substantial proportion of their unemployment is the result of a natural tendency to move frequently between school and work or from job to job during this transition period. Undoubtedly some youth unemployment is also the result of the failure of the number of jobs to expand sufficiently to absorb new entrants into the labor force, combined with the difficulty which new entrants have in finding employment when an increasing proportion of existing jobs is effectively reserved for their incumbents on the basis of seniority. But what stands out most starkly in the data is the high and growing incidence of joblessness among minority youth, especially those from low-income families or inner city neighborhoods. It is here where the problem seems to be most clearly structural in nature and where a more intensive effort to ease the problem is badly needed.

In short, if unemployment and lack of labor force participation among minority youth is "the problem," then policy solutions argue strongly for highly specialized and carefully targeted programs for that group. Indeed, if one interprets the problem as limited largely to low-income minority youth, located primarily in the inner cities of urban areas, the target population might not exceed perhaps 500,000 persons nationwide.

However, we should be cautious about our ability to *quickly* eradicate the higher rate of unemployment among low-income minority youth. We do not even fully understand the reasons for their joblessness. The problem can be traced in part to early home environment, poor schooling, and the other disadvantages found in low-income communities, but is also due to the concentration of minorities in areas where there are few jobs and to the availability of other sources of income.

It is likely that overt racial discrimination has declined during the past several decades, but the refusal to hire minority youth because of biased employer perceptions concerning the attitudes, behavior, and capabilities of minorities continues to be a serious problem. As indicated by Eli Anderson in a previous chapter, some black youth display hostile and antagonistic attitudes toward white employers and often bring to the workplace patterns of behavior markedly different from that consistent with middle-class values. The unfavorable reaction of employers to such attitudes and behavior on the part of some black youth undoubtedly affects employer perceptions of all black youth, thereby reducing the probability that a black youth will be hired in any available job vacancy. The magnitude of this problem is difficult to measure, but when added to the other economic and social barriers to employment, its impact is likely to be substantial.

From Analysis to Solution

To a considerable extent, the absence of a consensus on the nature and dimensions of the youth employment problem exacerbates the identification and selection of policy options for the immediate years ahead. If the problem is defined as a shortfall of jobs below the number of active and potential members of the youth labor force, then the appropriate policy option will be job creation. Either public job creation or public incentives for private job creation might be used to expand the total number of employment opportunities for youth.

On the other hand, if one views "the problem" as negative attitudes, inadequate basic skills, and nonproductive behavior on the part of youth themselves, the most appropriate policy solution would be one that emphasizes improvements in youth employability and socialization, including remedial education, training, counseling, work experience, improved labor market information, and similar measures. Such measures are designed to narrow the gap between the job preparation of youth and the expectations of employers. The fact that a variety of strategies has been tried in the past reflects the complexity of the problem; no single approach is likely to be successful. However, legislation, including YEDPA, has not always been consistent with what evidence is available on the nature and scope of the problem and on the impact of employment and training programs. As a result, public funds devoted to youth employment programs often are not used to best advantage and may contribute less than is hoped to an amelioration of the problem.

While any new set of programs should be more carefully tailored to what is known about their likely effectiveness, policy choices will need to be made in the face of incomplete understanding. In the remainder of this chapter, we provide our best judgments on what some of these choices should be. These judgments reflect not only our own views, but also those of many of the participants at the American Assembly held at Arden House in August of 1979.

The Policy Challenge Ahead

In our view, the cutting edge of "the problem" of youth employment is the persistent labor market difficulties of low-income, minority youth, many of whom are concentrated in distressed urban and rural areas. Our goal over the next decade should be to improve the labor market prospects of these youth so that there is (a) a long-term improvement in their employment and earnings, (b) a narrowing of the differential employment prospects of minority group and other youth, and (c) a decline in overall youth joblessness. A variety of approaches is required to achieve this goal, but the main elements of a youth employment policy for the 1980s might be (a) greater targeting of resources, (b) more emphasis on *selective* job creation, (c) improved forms of work experience and training, (d) better linkages between education and work, and (e) a greater role for the private sector.

Targeting of Resources

Today there is increasing recognition that the most efficient way to deal with structural problems in the labor market is to concentrate available resources on the people and places in greatest need. This philosophy was reflected in the reenacted CETA legislation and in earlier policies on public works spending and community development block grants. Similarly, in order to maximize the impact of limited funds available for youth employment purposes, increased efforts must be made to identify the demographic groups in greatest need, the areas in which they are located, and the most effective administrative arrangements for delivering the jobs and employability development services they need.

While the benefits of targeting are fully appreciated, the design of measures that will increase targeting has proven to be very difficult. It is clear that generalized funding practices, based on broadly defined formulas and tied to unemployment statistics, do not result either in a distribution of funds or a selection of program services most appropriate for reducing the labor market difficulties of youth. Such generalized formulas often divert funds to places where the problem of youth unemployment is less serious than in hard-pressed urban and rural areas. Also, the use of generalized formulas, by making political jurisdictions eligible for receipt of funds, may truncate the development of interorganizational cooperation, such as that between local education agencies and CETA prime sponsors, that can be very beneficial in the design and implementation of effective program strategies. Although much can be said for the apparent objectivity of formula funding practices, much more can be said for measures that target more of the available funds directly on the most seriously disadvantaged youth.

The achievement of better resource targeting is also related to the selection of service deliverers. The goal should be to identify and support the program operators with the best potential for reaching and providing effective services to youth designated for high priority assistance.

In some cases, this will mean working through the CETA system, much as is done today. In other cases, however, it might be necessary to go beyond the CETA system to enlist the cooperation, or expand the participation, of organizations other than CETA prime sponsors. Included among institutions whose role might be enlarged are secondary school systems, community colleges, and community based organizations. It is desirable to have multiple service deliverers at the local level so that youth will have options which meet their specific needs.

Selective Job Creation

Some have argued that with higher than average levels of unemployment among adults, it is unlikely that much, if anything, can be done to reduce youth unemployment. By emphasizing the youth unemployment rate, this view of the problem may be too limited, but beyond that, there is the implication that economic stimulus is the correct policy solution.

Rarely, if ever, has economic stimulation been pursued for the express purpose of creating more jobs for youth. Adult unemployment above acceptable levels usually provides the motive force for measures to stimulate the economy. As the economy moves toward full employment, the position of youth improves both absolutely and relatively to adults, but the offsetting factor in the recent past has been the worsening of inflationary pressures. Also, the unemployment rates of minority youth remain at depression levels even when the economy approaches full employment. For these reasons, generalized policies directed toward further lowering of the aggregate unemployment rate cannot be the major vehicle for improving the position of youth in the labor market. On the other hand, any worsening of job prospects for adults will surely limit employment opportunities for youth. A high-employment economy is a necessary, if not a sufficient, prerequisite for reducing youth unemployment.

A more selective approach to generating youth employment opportunities is a necessary addition to maintaining high levels of employment in the economy at large. Because much of the joblessness among minority youth is highly localized and reflects, to some extent, serious weaknesses in local economies, special devices are required to encourage job creation in areas of greatest need. Targeted employment tax credits, and project-oriented public service employment can help achieve selective job creation goals. These selective job creation devices would tend to minimize the inflationary effects of public expenditures and would be more consistent with the targeting of scarce resources.

Equal opportunities for youth can also be generated by more effective efforts to coordinate federal assistance grants at the local level. At the present time, the federal government provides a wide range of grants to local communities to assist them in promoting local economic development, improved housing, better transportation systems, and other purposes. When viewed together with funds available for employment and training programs, the federal assistance grants represent a formidable array of resources that can be useful in attacking the youth unemployment problem.

Unfortunately, the potential benefits for youth employment from the combined use of federal assistance grants to local communities are reduced by conflicting program regulations, inadequate planning systems, and other barriers to full coordination of such funds. Greater job creation for youth might be achieved if ways can be found to coordinate the expenditure of CETA, urban development block grants, community development block grants, and local public work funds, to mention a few of the major federal assistance programs. Since youth, especially minority youth, are disproportionately represented among the unemployed in many areas, youth employment should be raised to a higher level on the list of priorities among goals to be achieved from federal assistance grants to local communities.

Improved Forms of Training and Work Experience

No strategy for addressing youth labor market difficulties can ignore the importance of employability development. The key question is what type of employability development (and what combination of program services) will be most effective?

Experience under CETA and previous manpower development legislation shows that youth deficiencies in basic education often reduce the effectiveness of short-term skills training programs. The average duration for participation in CETA programs is about six months. It is unlikely that the accumulated effects of poor basic education can be overcome and marketable job skills acquired in that period of time. In order to provide disadvantaged youth with competencies to prepare for better job opportunities, training programs need to be lengthened and to place greater emphasis on remedial communication and computational skills.

Equally important, employability development programs should be designed with recognition that occupational change is likely to be frequent in the economy of the 1980s. Those persons most capable of adjusting to frequent changes in occupational requirements may well be the ones who experience the least unemployment over time. For these reasons, classroom training programs should not overemphasize development of skills limited to narrow occupations. It would be more desirable to focus on job skills applicable to a range of occupations within a career field.

Some consideration should also be given to an expansion of on-the-job training and apprenticeship programs. Many employers much prefer to provide their own training and ask only that youth who are hired bring a minimum acceptable level of basic education and a positive attitude toward work. Company-specific training might reduce the potential for occupational mobility among youth, but it has the advantage of providing a direct link between training and employment. This can be very important to the disadvantaged, many of whom have limited motivation because they see little connection between their participation in a training program and a job at the end of the line.

Increasing employability also requires a serious review of work experience programs. If anything, too much emphasis has been placed on work experience, and too little on training and remedial education. But the work experience provided can be much improved. Much of current work experience for youth is part-time employment in menial jobs offering little more than a holding station while the aging process occurs. Work experience can be of no value if the environment in which it takes place bears little relationship to real life work requirements. Good supervision, adherence to reasonable work standards, penalties for poor work performance, rewards for exemplary performance, all contribute to a valuable work experience that can have important benefits for later full-time, unsubsidized employment. Unfortunately, students of employment and training programs have little knowledge about how to develop good work habits and positive attitudes toward work among those youth who enter the labor market with serious attitudinal and behavioral handicaps. Continued experimentation with alternative types of work experience programs operating in different employer settings, and with community based organizations which stress better socialization of youth will add to the fund of knowledge on which further improvements in such employability development efforts can be made.

Better Linkage Between Education and Work

The search for more effective strategies for dealing with youth employment problems in the years ahead will lead inevitably toward a larger role for public school systems. Unquestionably, the schools will have to play a stronger role in preparing youth for the job market. Greater progress must be made in improving the quality of basic education, especially in urban inner city schools. The school system is the key public institution in our society responsible for preparing youth with both basic skills and with knowledge of and readiness for work. The schools should be held accountable for effectively performing their roles, particularly for those youth who will not go on to higher education. The schools may need to place greater emphasis on labor market related curricula and programs, especially for youths aged fourteen to seventeen. If in-school youth can be helped more effectively, fewer will become disadvantaged adults.

Employment counseling services in the schools should be strengthened and transformed to include job development and job placement. There should be greater contact between employment counselors and potential employers. These employment counselors should develop a wider knowledge of the training, work, and educational options available to youth. Greater efforts should also be made to teach young people how to identify and pursue available job opportunities. At the same time, the occupational training should be supplemented by labor market information to insure that youth develop both marketable skills and the knowledge and ability to use the most effective methods to identify and pursue available job opportunities.

Although most youth can benefit from programs in established schools, some youth will be better served in educational facilities which operate outside the traditional school setting. In recent years there have been special experiments with alternative schools in New York City, Philadelphia, and Oakland, California. These experiments have demonstrated both the potential and the limitations of such institutions. On balance, however, the evidence supports the conclusion that alternative schools can reach and serve some segments of the urban youth population that would otherwise leave school and drift into joblessness. The evidence also suggests, however, that such institutions work best when they maintain some connection with the established school system in local communities. The alternative schools should be carefully monitored and held accountable for effectiveness in basic skill development and work preparation. Moreover, employers should be actively involved in this process in order to gain their acceptance of it.

A Greater Role for the Private Sector

In searching for more effective ways to reduce youth labor market difficulties, attention must be given to the appropriate role of both the public and private sectors. At the present time, public employment and training programs represent by far the major opportunities for work and training among disadvantaged youth. Indeed, some analysts have suggested that all the employment gains for black youth during 1978 were attributable to YEDPA programs. Although that claim is questionable, there is no doubt that public programs occupy center stage in current efforts to deal with youth unemployment.

Changes in the employment base of many communities as a result of industrial relocation and regional disparities in the rate of economic growth mean that public job creation programs, carefully targeted to areas where jobs are scarce, will continue to be necessary in any strategy to help disadvantaged youth.

At the present time, however, intervention strategies are weighted too heavily in the direction of public job creation programs. One disadvantage of the current mix of strategies is that private sector initiatives have been crowded out in many communities because public sector initiatives play such a dominant role in local efforts to expand job opportunities for youth. For example, in small communities with limited public sector capacity for providing work experiences for youth, available funds under CETA often cannot be fully utilized because local prime sponsors are prohibited from using federal funds to support employment opportunities in the private sector. Some urban prime sponsors also face similar problems, especially in planning summer youth employment programs.

There may be valuable payoffs from efforts to expand employment opportunities for youth in the private sector, especially in locations where labor demand is increasing and where the pool of unemployed, experienced adults is limited. Expanded experimentation with private sector-oriented programs, such as those which utilize tax credits for employment, reductions in social security contributions, special referral services for youth workers, and expanded school year and summer work experience opportunities in the private sector, can produce valuable evidence on ways to enlist the resources of the private sector in hiring and training more youth. Although there are many problems of implementation, subsidies which reduce the cost of hiring youth may be as effective as public employment programs in creating jobs. An additional advantage of this approach is that it offers direct entry into the sector of the economy where the vast majority of jobs, both now and in the future, will be located.

In the last several years, there have been several attempts to shift the balance of program mix toward greater private sector participation. Under YEDPA, for example, 100 percent wage subsidies have been offered the private sector to place disadvantaged youth between the ages of sixteen and nineteen in part-time and summer jobs under the entitlement program. Reasonably successful results with this experiment have been reported in Baltimore, Philadelphia, and several other cities in which the entitlement program now operates.

Another attempt to encourage more private sector participation is the Targeted Jobs Tax Credit. Passed in 1978, this legislation provides up to a 50 percent subsidy for employers who hire disadvantaged youth. Designed to reduce the unemployment of youth and other hard-to-employ groups, this device is a targeted version of the New Jobs Tax Credit enacted in 1977 as a countercyclical device to stimulate job creation. It is too early to evaluate its effectiveness, but federal policy makers hope it will fill some of the gap created by cut-backs in funding for PSE programs.

Certainly, the private sector offers no panacea in the search for solutions to youth employment problems. Experience with the National Alliance of Businessmen/Job Opportunities in the Business Sector (NAB/JOBS) program during the past decade demonstrates the difficulties involved in launching and sustaining an effective private sector effort to expand employment opportunities for disadvantaged youth. Recent efforts to reorganize Private Industry Councils (PIC) under Title VII of CETA also reveal the difficulties in forging a link between CETA prime sponsors and the private sector to have a direct impact on jobs for youth. Under the aegis of PICs, local employers are encouraged to examine the hiring standards and employment needs in order to identify more opportunities for the disadvantaged. A special effort is being made to enlist the cooperation of small and mid-sized employers who, in the past, did not participate widely in government sponsored employment and training efforts.

The early experience with this new private sector initiative offers a mixed picture of employer willingness to play a larger role in youth employment efforts. The early experiences also show, however, that purposive and determined efforts, in which participation of the private sector in planning as well as implementation is maximized, can produce innovative and effective responses to youth employment problems. The efforts are not limited to PICs. For example, an especially interesting case of corporate commitment undertaken without public incentives is the pledge by David Mahoney of Norton Simon Company to hire ten minority youth for every thousand employees during the next year (1979–80). Similarly, the Xerox Corporation donated $500,000 to the U.S. Department of Labor to be used to hire disadvantaged youth in selected communities around the nation. The task immediately ahead is to enlarge upon the models of success and provide support for promising ventures through which public and private funds can be used to leverage more private sector initiatives in pursuit of greater employment opportunities for youth.

Summary and Conclusion

Given the magnitude of the challenge and the cumulative disadvantages which stem from family, school, and community, and the stickiness of the unemployment rate even in the face of expanding job opportunities, it would be unrealistic to expect a large reduction in youth unemployment or an elimination of racial disparities at an early date. Any new policies for youth should probably be designed to improve both their immediate employment prospects and their long-term employability, with the balance between the two varying with age and individual circumstance. It will not be possible, and may not be desirable, to reduce youth unemployment to the levels experienced by adults. Nevertheless, there are some long-term benefits to be derived from an added investment in the nation's youth, and these benefits alone may justify special federal efforts to improve their position in the labor market.

Within the youth population, attention needs to be given to the especially disadvantaged status of minorities. The evidence in previous chapters suggests that they have both the greatest employability needs and the greatest difficulty obtaining jobs, even when they are fully prepared to take on productive roles.

The success of any new efforts will depend critically on the wisdom with which they are designed and implemented. The challenge is great, and the task will be difficult. This is not a time, however, to despair of the future. If the labor market problem of youth is approached with commitment and determination, and if carefully defined and realistic goals are established, there is no reason to believe effective solutions through public policy cannot be found.

Index

Affirmative action programs, 65
Age discrimination laws, 24
Agriculture, decline of, 13
Aid to Families with Dependent Children (AFDC), 45, 106
Alcoholism, 28
Alienation, 64, 80, 83, 86, 113, 141
Aliens, 27, 74
Alternative schools, 152
Anderson, Bernard E., 1-5, 137-55
Anderson, Elijah, 2, 64-87, 126, 145
Apprenticeships, 129-30, 150
Ashenfelter, Orley, 99, 104-5, 106
Australia, 116, 117, 120, 121, 130

Baby boom cohort, 2, 12, 15, 25, 27, 44, 60, 120-21
Banfield, Edward, 67
Barclay, Suzanne, 96
Baugh, John, 69
Becker, Howard S., 84
Bedrosian, Hrach, 24
Belgium, 125, 131, 132
Bilingual education, 119
Black Cultural Nationalism, 68
Black Panthers, 67
Black self-concept, 64-66, 68-70, 76
Black separatism, 68, 70
Black youth unemployment, 64-87, 89
    discrimination, 24, 66
    employment/population ratio, 26-28, 29, 58-59, 61, 89, 107
    female unemployment rates, 3, 89
    growth of, 26-27
    job aspirations, 78-81
    rates, 35-37
    residual rates, 55
    school enrollment rates, 58-59, 61
    serial unemployment, 76-78, 82
    underground economy, 81-87
    U3 measure of, 52-53
    wage rates, 20-21, 27, 58

Brown, Charles, 23
Brown, H. Rap, 67
Brown, James, 68
Bureau of Labor Statistics (BLS), 15, 34, 39
    unemployment rate, 49-52, 61

Cain, Glen G., 103
Canada, 116, 120-23, 130
Career Services system, 18
Carmichael, Stokely, 67
CETA (see Comprehensive Employment and Training Act programs)
Childbearing, 53, 55
Civil Rights movement, 65, 67-70, 85
Clark, Kim B., 17, 19, 20, 117
Competitive labor, 14
Comprehensive Employment and Training Act (CETA) programs, 98, 139, 147-50, 153, 154
Confidence games, 82
Cooperative vocational education program, 101
Crime, 24, 28, 64, 66, 82-84, 86, 91, 141
Cross-area evidence, 15
Cross-sectional data, 15
Current Population Survey (CPS), 15, 16
Cyclical unemployment, 37-38, 40-48, 60, 119-20

Demand and supply factors, 9, 12-14, 89
Denmark, 128, 135
Diamond, Daniel E., 24
Discrimination, 12, 13, 24, 66, 72-73, 89, 145
Dropouts, 49, 53
Drug abuse, 28, 82

Education, 38, 49-53, 55, 57, 60, 142-44, 151-52
  enrollment rates, 49, 52, 58-59, 61
  foreign, 118
Employability development programs, 149-51
Employer discrimination, 12, 13, 24, 66, 72-73, 89, 145
Employment counseling services, 151
Employment/population ratio, 8-11, 19, 22, 56-59
  black, 26-28, 29, 58-59, 61, 89, 107
Employment tax credits, 48, 60, 149, 153
Entry rate unemployment, 17-18
Equal opportunity laws, 24
Equilibrium unemployment rates, 42-44, 47, 48, 56, 60
European Community (E.C.), 114, 116
Expansionary monetary and fiscal policies, 38, 40-42

Fackler, James S., 101
Family background, 21
Family income, 21, 39, 45, 46, 56, 78
Female labor force participation rates, 44, 121-22
Female youth unemployment rates, 2-3, 36, 53-54, 89, 114
Fencing, 82
Fertility rates, 55
Food Stamp Program, 39, 45
Foreign youth unemployment, 112-35
  baby boom cohorts and, 120-21
  factors in, 119-27
  female labor force participation and, 121-22
  income transfers, 125-26
  job changing and, 126 27
  minimum wage and, 122-24
  programs, 127-35
  trends in, 114-19
France, 116, 117, 122, 124, 128, 131-32
Freeman, Richard B., 2, 3, 6-29, 89, 116, 124, 125
Frictional unemployment, 37

Gangs, 80
GED certification, 97
General Accounting Office (GAO), 102
Germany, 116-18, 128-30
Ginzberg, Eli, 5

Goffman, Erving, 79
Gramlich, Edward M., 23
Great Britain, 18, 119-21, 125, 126, 128, 129, 131, 133-34

Hayden, Tom, 67
Help-wanted ads, 23
Higginbotham, Leon, 70
High school dropouts, 49, 53
Holland, 114, 118, 122-25, 129, 131, 132, 134
Hughes, Everett C., 71
Humphrey-Hawkins legislation, 40

Illegal aliens, 27, 74
Income transfers, 125-26
Inflation, 40-42, 60
In-kind transfers, 45
Institutional training, 104-6
Ireland, 131
Italy, 113, 116, 117

Jackson, Jesse, 68
Janowitz, Morris, 67
Japan, 116, 117, 120, 122
Job aspirations, 12, 78-81
Job attachment, 56, 61
Job changing, 126-27
Job Corps, 95, 97, 98, 103, 108, 138, 140
Job creation programs, 129-30, 148-49, 152-54
Joblessness index, 55-56, 61
Jobs, availability of, 12, 22-23
JOBS program, 98
Johnson, Lyndon B., 67

Kennedy, John F., 67
Kennedy-Johnson tax cut, 40
Keynesian unemployment (*see* Cyclical unemployment)
Kiefer, Nicholas M., 104, 105
Killingworth, Charles, 41
King, Martin Luther, Jr., 65, 67

Labor, Department of, 154
Labor force participation rates, 44, 121-22
Layoffs, 17, 38, 47
Leighton, Linda, 19
Longitudinal data, 16

Mahoney, David, 154
Malcolm X, 68
Mallar, Charles, 91, 103, 104
Mangum, Garth, 92, 98, 100, 102-4
Manpower Development and Training
    Act (MDTA), 41
Manpower Services Commission (Great
    Britain), 119-20
Manpower training, 48, 60
Marshall, Ray, 137
Marston, Stephen, 19
Maynard, Rebecca, 106
Media stereotypes, 66, 71
Medoff, James, 16
Merton, Robert K., 73, 82
Military service, 26, 41, 48, 49
Mincer, Jacob, 19, 23
Minimum wage, 12, 13, 23, 39, 44-46,
    77, 122-24
Mobility, 12, 13, 19, 24, 29, 51
Mooney, Joseph D., 100
Muhammed, Elijah, 68

NAIRU (nonaccelerating-inflation rate
    of unemployment), 42-44, 47, 48,
    56, 60
National Alliance of Businessmen/Job
    Opportunities in the Business
    Sector (NAB/JOBS) program,
    154
National Longitudinal Survey, 141
National Supported Work Demonstra-
    tion, 106, 108
Neighborhood Youth Corps (NYC), 41,
    100-102
Nelson, Clifford, 5
Netherlands, 114, 118, 122-25, 129, 131,
    132, 134
New Jobs Tax Credit of 1977, 154
New Zealand, 120, 121
Nixon, Richard M., 103
Norton Simon Company, 154

On-the-job training, 12, 38, 93, 106,
    150
Organization for Economic Cooperation
    and Development (OECD), 129,
    132, 137

Parental income, 21, 39, 45, 46, 56, 78
Parks, Rosa, 67

Part-time work, 39, 40, 48, 49, 57, 59,
    60
Perry, Charles R., 98
Pickpocketing, 82
Pilot Projects, 140
Pimping, 82
Pitcher, Hugh M., 100
Portugal, 122, 124
Prime-age unemployment, 36-38, 52
Private Industry Councils (PIC), 154
Public service employment, 149

Quits, 17, 47

Racial pride, 68-70
Ragan, James J., Jr., 23
Recessions, 40, 41
Recruitment Subsidy for School-leavers
    (Great Britain), 133
Reservation wage, 22-23
Residual unemployment rates, 53-56
Reubens, Beatrice G., 3, 112-35
Riots, 65, 67, 85
Robbery, 82
Robin, Gerald G., 101

Sawhill, Isabel V., 1-5, 137-55
School dropouts, 49, 53
School enrollment rates, 49, 52, 58-59,
    61
Schooling (*see* Education)
Self-concept, black, 64-66, 68-70, 76
Self-fulfilling prophecy, 73, 77
Seniority, 12-13, 19, 38
Serial unemployment, 76-78, 82
Sit-ins, 67
Skill levels, 12, 13, 38, 39, 48, 49, 56,
    60
Smith, Robert S., 100
Socioeconomic status, 19-21, 24
Somers, Gerald G., 100-101
Stack, Carol, 78
Standard Metropolitan Statistical Areas
    (SMSA), 22
Stealing, 77
Stereotypes, black, 66, 71
Stromsdorfer, Ernst W., 4, 88-109
Structural unemployment, 37-38, 60,
    119-20
Suburbanization of jobs, 26

Summer Program for Economically Dis-
    advantaged Youth (SPEDY), 102,
    108
Summer Program for Employment of
    Disadvantaged Youth, 97
Summers, Lawrence H., 17, 19, 20, 117
Summer work, 39, 40, 95, 97, 102, 108,
    138, 153
Summer Youth Employment Program,
    95, 97, 102, 138
Supply and demand factors, 9, 12-14, 89
Sweden, 116, 117, 121, 128, 135

Taggart, Robert, III, 98
Targeted Jobs Tax Credit of 1978, 153-
    54
Teenage pregnancy, 141
Temporary   Employment   Subsidy
    (Great Britain), 130
Temporary jobs, 12, 13
Tenure, 19
Tight labor markets, 41
Time series evidence, 15
Turnover, 12, 13, 23, 24, 29

Underground economy, 12, 81-87
Unemployment:
    cyclical, 37-38, 40-48, 60, 119-20
    frictional, 37
    prime-age, 36-38, 52
    serial, 76-78, 82
    structural, 37-38, 60, 119-20
    (*see also* Unemployment rates; Youth
        unemployment)
Unemployment rates:
    defined, 34-35, 39
    equilibrium, 42-44, 47, 48, 56, 60
    inflation and, 40-42, 60
    residual, 53-56
    zero cyclical, 42, 43, 46-48, 60
Unified Vocational Preparation Scheme
    (Great Britain), 128
U1 measure of unemployment, 49-52,
    61
U2 measure of unemployment, 49-53
U3 measure of unemployment, 50-53

Vocational education, 91-92, 101

Voluntary unemployment, 39

Wachter, Michael L., 2, 4, 33-61, 89,
    117, 124, 125
Wage aspirations, 12, 13
Wages:
    of blacks, 20-21, 27, 58
    decline in youth, relative to older
        workers, 25
    minimum, 12, 13, 23, 39, 44-46, 77,
        122-24
Wage-theft system, 77
Walsh, John, 92, 98, 100, 102-4
Welfare, 27-28, 39, 45, 46
Westcott, D., 26
Wilson, William J., 66, 80
Wise, David, 16, 17, 19, 22, 23, 27
Work ethic, 12, 13, 84
Work Experience Program (Great Brit-
    ain), 133, 134

Xerox Corporation, 154

Young Adult Conservation Corps
    (YACC), 93, 94, 140
Youth Act of 1977, 89, 104
Youth Community Conservation and
    Improvement Projects, 93, 94,
    140
Youth Employment and Demonstration
    Projects Act (YEDPA), 138, 140,
    143, 146, 152, 153
Youth Employment and Training Pro-
    grams, 95, 97, 140
Youth Employment Subsidy (Great
    Britain), 133
Youth Incentive Entitlement Pilot
    Projects, 93, 94, 96-97, 98, 100,
    101, 108
Youth Opportunities Program (Great
    Britain), 128, 133, 134
Youth programs, 88-109, 138-40, 146-54
    design of, 93-98
    displacement, problem of, 106-7
    evaluation of antecedents of, 100-106
    foreign, 127-35
    past experience with, 98-99
    rationales for, 90-93
Youth subminimum wage, 48

Youth unemployment:
alternative methods for measuring, 48-59
causes of, 6-29
cyclical factors in, 40-48
foreign (*see* Foreign youth unemployment)
high rates of, 39-40

Youth unemployment (*cont.*)
minority (*see* Black youth unemployment)
policy approaches for future, 137-55
programs (*see* Youth programs)

Zero cyclical unemployment, 42, 43, 46-48, 60

The American Assembly

About The American Assembly

The American Assembly was established by Dwight D. Eisenhower at Columbia University in 1950. It holds nonpartisan meetings and publishes authoritative books to illuminate issues of United States policy.

An affiliate of Columbia, with offices in the Graduate School of Business, the Assembly is a national educational institution incorporated in the State of New York.

The Assembly seeks to provide information, stimulate discussion, and evoke independent conclusions in matters of vital public interest.

AMERICAN ASSEMBLY SESSIONS

At least two national programs are initiated each year. Authorities are retained to write background papers presenting essential data and defining the main issues in each subject.

A group of men and women representing a broad range of experience, competence, and American leadership meet for several days to discuss the Assembly topic and consider alternatives for national policy.

All Assemblies follow the same procedure. The background papers are sent to participants in advance of the Assembly. The Assembly meets in small groups for four or five lengthy periods. All groups use the same agenda. At the close of these informal sessions, participants adopt in plenary sessions a final report of findings and recommendations.

Regional, state, and local Assemblies are held following the national session at Arden House. Assemblies have also been held in England, Switzerland, Malaysia, Canada, the Caribbean, South America, Central America, the Philippines, and Japan. Over one hundred thirty institutions have co-sponsored one or more Assemblies.

ARDEN HOUSE

Home of the American Assembly and scene of the national sessions is Arden House, which was given to Columbia University in 1950 by W. Averell Harriman. E. Roland Harriman joined his brother in contributing toward adaptation of the property for conference purposes. The buildings and surrounding land, known as the Harriman Campus of Columbia University, are 50 miles north of New York City.

Arden House is a distinguished conference center. It is self-supporting and operates throughout the year for use by organizations with educational objectives.

AMERICAN ASSEMBLY BOOKS

The background papers for each Assembly are published in cloth and paperbound editions for use by individuals, libraries, businesses, public agencies, nongovernmental organizations, educational institutions, discussion and service groups. In this way the deliberations of Assembly sessions are continued and extended.

The subject of Assembly programs to date are:

1951——United States-Western Europe Relationships
1952——Inflation
1953——Economic Security for Americans
1954——The United States' Stake in the United Nations
——The Federal Government Service
1955——United States Agriculture
——The Forty-Eight States
1956——The Representation of the United States Abroad
——The United States and the Far East
1957——International Stability and Progress
——Atoms for Power
1958——The United States and Africa
——United States Monetary Policy
1959——Wages, Prices, Profits, and Productivity
——The United States and Latin America
1960——The Federal Government and Higher Education
— –The Secretary of State
——Goals for Americans
1961——Arms Control: Issues for the Public
——Outer Space: Prospects for Man and Society
1962——Automation and Technological Change
——Cultural Affairs and Foreign Relations
1963——The Population Dilemma
——The United States and the Middle East

1964——The United States and Canada
    ——The Congress and America's Future
1965——The Courts, the Public, and the Law Explosion
    ——The United States and Japan
1966——State Legislatures in American Politics
    ——A World of Nuclear Powers?
    ——The United States and the Philippines
    ——Challenges to Collective Bargaining
1967——The United States and Eastern Europe
    ——Ombudsmen for American Government?
1968——Uses of the Seas
    ——Law in a Changing America
    ——Overcoming World Hunger
1969——Black Economic Development
    ——The States and the Urban Crisis
1970——The Health of Americans
    ——The United States and the Caribbean
1971——The Future of American Transportation
    ——Public Workers and Public Unions
1972——The Future of Foundations
    ——Prisoners in America
1973——The Worker and the Job
    ——Choosing the President
1974——The Good Earth of America
    ——On Understanding Art Museums
    ——Global Companies
1975——Law and the American Future
    ——Women and the American Economy
1976——Nuclear Power Controversy
    ——Jobs for Americans
    ——Capital for Productivity and Jobs
1977——The Ethics of Corporate Conduct
    ——The Performing Arts and American Society
1978——Running the American Corporation
    ——Race for the Presidency
    ——Energy Conservation and Public Policy
1979——Disorders in Higher Education
    ——Youth Employment and Public Policy
1980——The Economy and the President
    ——Farms into Cities

Second Editions, Revised:

1962——The United States and the Far East
1963——The United States and Latin America
    ——The United States and Africa
1964——United States Monetary Policy
1965——The Federal Government Service
    ——The Representation of the United States Abroad
1968——Cultural Affairs and Foreign Relations
    ——Outer Space: Prospects for Man and Society
1969——The Population Dilemma
1973——The Congress and America's Future
1975——The United States and Japan